西安交通大学"十四五"规划教材
西安交通大学少年班规划教材·英语

BRIDGE TO COLLEGE

阅读与写作(2)

READING AND WRITING FOR ACADEMIC STUDY

牛莉◎总主编

成旻 龚颖◎本册主编

成旻 龚颖 牛莉◎编者

西安交通大学出版社

XI'AN JIAOTONG UNIVERSITY PRESS

图书在版编目(CIP)数据

阅读与写作. 2 / 牛莉总主编；成旻，龚颖本册主编. —西安：
西安交通大学出版社，2021.3(2025.8重印)
西安交通大学少年班规划教材.英语
ISBN 978 - 7 - 5605 - 6011 - 3

Ⅰ.①阅… Ⅱ.①牛… ②成… ③龚… Ⅲ.①英语－阅读教学－
高等学校－教材 ②英语－写作－高等学校－教材 Ⅳ.①H319.39

中国版本图书馆 CIP 数据核字(2020)第 132597 号

书　　名	阅读与写作(2)	
总 主 编	牛　莉	
本册主编	成　旻　龚　颖	
责任编辑	李　蕊	

出版发行	西安交通大学出版社
	(西安市兴庆南路 1 号　邮政编码 710048)
网　　址	http://www.xjtupress.com
电　　话	(029)82668357　82667874(市场营销中心)
	(029)82668315(总编办)
传　　真	(029)82668280
印　　刷	西安五星印刷有限公司

开　　本	710mm×1000mm　1/16	印　张	10.125	字　数	251 千字
版次印次	2021 年 3 月第 1 版　　2025 年 8 月第 4 次印刷				
书　　号	ISBN 978 - 7 - 5605 - 6011 - 3				
定　　价	38.00 元				

如发现印装质量问题,请与本社市场营销中心联系。
订购热线:(029)82665248　(029)82667874
投稿热线:(029)82668531　(029)82665371
读者信箱:xjtu_rw@163.com

总序
Foreword

　　1985 年对西安交通大学来说是一个值得铭记的年份。这一年,教育部正式批准学校开办少年班,学校积极响应邓小平同志的指示:"在人才的问题上,要特别强调一下,必须打破常规去发现、选拔和培养杰出的人才。"转眼间,少年班已走过了三十五年的办学历程,在破解"如何发现智力超常少年并因材施教"这一极具挑战性的难题上,西安交通大学先后有五位校长,他们艰难探索,矢志不渝,构建了一套适合中国国情且自主创新的少年班人才选拔和培养体系,培养了一批又一批少年英才。目前,少年班从初中应届毕业生中选拔招生,实行"预科一本科一硕士"八年制贯通培养模式,其中,预科一年级在指定的四所优秀预科中学学习,预科二年级在大学学习,各为期一年。

　　基础教育与高等教育的有机衔接一直是少年班探索和研究的重点,而教材作为知识衔接的重要载体,成为影响少年班教育质量的关键因素。为此,钱学森学院于 2010 年 10 月成立少年班教材编写小组,正式启动教材编写研究工作。全国首套少年班系列教材于 2014 年 12 月出版,来自大学及高中的近 60 名专家和一线教师参与其中,谨遵"因材施教,发掘潜能,注重创新,超常教育,培养英才"的指导思想,通过多次研讨、仔细斟酌、反复修订和严格审核,耗时四年有余,最终编写并出版了全国首套将"预科一本科"有机衔接的教材。这套教材包含六门课程,共 22 种,总计 2550 学时,828 万字。这套教材自出版至今,使用效果良好。

　　2018 年,经过大量调研,钱学森学院制定了新版少年班培养方案,在新版培养方案的基础上规划修订数学、物理、化学、英语等课程的教材,并于 2020 年启动少年班"十四五"规划教材的编写出版工作。此版教材将力求实现"预科一本科"课程的无缝衔接,从知识体系、内容结构、案例设计、习题配套等方面对教材内涵和风格进行重新编撰和优化,同时注重拔尖学生的发展需求,体现新版少年班培养方案中"以兴趣为导向"的教育教学改革思想。

　　愿此版教材可让更多关注少年班的有识之士受益。同时,我们也希望借此机会,号召大家集思广益,群策群力,共同为推动少年英才培养进程做出努力。

　　是为序。

杨　森

2020 年 8 月 10 日

从 2012 年开始接手少年班的教学工作,我们的教学团队一直在探索适合少年班的英语教学模式,包括课程设置、教学内容、教学方法与手段、评价方式及教材等。2018 年我校钱学森学院重新制定了少年班培养方案,我们团队也借此机会对我们的教学模式重新进行了梳理,决定开设两门英语课程:"阅读与写作(Reading and Writing for Academic Study)"和"交流与表达(Communication for Academic Study)"。因此,为这两门课程而编写的两套同名教材应运而生。同时,基于少年班英语课程培养方案的总目标,即"帮助学生完成从通用英语(English for General Purpose,EGP)到学术英语(English for Academic Study,EAS)的过渡,为学生进入大学学习做好语言能力的准备",我们又将这两套教材的编写内容进行了有机结合,构成了"通往大学"系列(Bridge to College)。

本系列教材有三个特色:

一、教材编写突出体现"以学习为中心"和"以成果为导向"的教学理念,如下图所示:

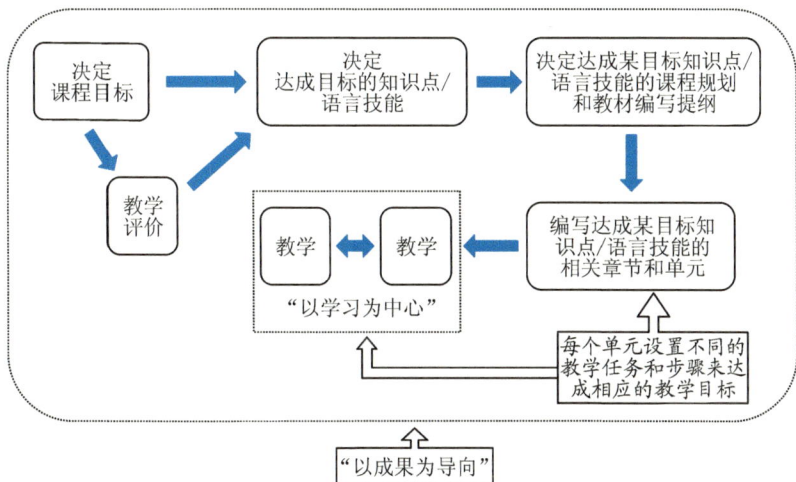

二、教材章节编排侧重构建英语语言知识和技能体系。与一般英语教材中以话题为章节(theme-based)的编写原则不同,本教材采用以功能为章节(function-based,即突出对语言知识点和技能的培养)的编写原则。因为,以话题为章节的编写理念侧重扩充相关话题的词汇量或表达,忽视了语言知识点或

语言技能之间的相关性，缺乏系统性，会导致学生在学习之后只能想起某些课文的内容；而本教材以功能为章节进行编写，其目的在于帮助学生获得相关知识点或技能，同时也帮助学生构建出完整的英语语言知识和技能体系。

三、教材内容融入教学设计。本教材中的各个章节，不仅是学生应掌握的相关知识点，同时也是教师在教学中的具体目标。本教材的章节编排突破了传统英语教材"课文＋练习"的模式，变为"通过设置不同的教学任务和步骤来达成相应的教学目标"的模式。这样的编写模式，既包含了学生学习的过程，也体现了教师教学的过程，实现了"以学习为中心"，即"教师为主导，学生为主体"的教学理念。

基于上述编写特点，本系列教材也适用于高中生和本科生自主学习。

最后，特别感谢各位编写老师牺牲难得的假期投入教材编写工作！特别感谢交大附中的刘晏辰老师对预科一年级教材讲义初稿的试用和及时的意见反馈！特别感谢少年班 2017 级、2018 级的同学们对教材讲义试用和新教学模式探索的积极配合和肯定！特别感谢西安交通大学钱学森学院和外国语学院给予我们团队的各种支持！特别感谢我们教学团队（包括各中学和大学的所有老师）的辛勤付出！

牛 莉
2020 年暑假

目 录
Table of Contents ▶

SECTION 1　　Writing a Good Paragraph(2)

Module 1　　Writing a Good Topic Sentence /003

Module 2　　Writing a Narrative Paragraph /015

Module 3　　Writing a Descriptive Paragraph /023

Module 4　　Writing an Expository Paragraph—Interpretation /032

Module 5　　Writing an Expository Paragraph—Classification and Extended-Definition /042

Module 6　　Writing an Expository Paragraph—Process /052

Module 7　　Writing an Expository Paragraph—Comparison and Contrast /060

Module 8　　Writing an Expository Paragraph—Cause AND Effect /070

Module 9　　Writing an Expository Paragraph—Problem-Solution /078

Module 10　Writing an Argumentative Paragraph /085

Module 11　Writing a Paragraph with Exemplification and Listing /094

SECTION 2　　Writing Letters for Practical Purposes

Module 12　Basic Elements and Formats of English Letters /107

Module 13　Writing Different Types of Friendly/Personal Letters /120

Module 14　Writing Different Types of Formal/Business Letters /129

Module 15　Writing Different Types of E-mails /139

List of Sources /151

SECTION 1

Writing a Good Paragraph (2)

Module 1 Writing a Good Topic Sentence

When finishing the learning of this module,

Goal 1   I will be able to write a good topic sentence.

Goal 2   I will know the functions of different paragraphs in an essay.

Goal 3   I will understand different puropses in paragraph writing.

Section 1   Writing a Good Paragraph (2)

TASK ONE
Writing a Good Topic Sentence

ACTIVITY 1 ▶

Understanding a good topic sentence

Step 1

Work in pairs and answer questions about the following paragraph.

I need a water bottle for the hike in case I get thirsty. A sweater is useful if it gets cold. A compass will help go in the right direction. Sandwiches will be an easy-to-carry snack. I can use a camera to take pictures of unusual or attractive places.

Questions:

1. What is the topic and the main idea of this paragraph?

2. Which of the following would be a good topic sentence of this paragraph?

(1) I will go bike riding on this weekend.

(2) I need many items to be ready for a safe, enjoyable hike.

(3) I bought many things for the weekend.

(4) My friend and I like taking pictures.

3. What is the use of a topic sentence to the writer and the reader?

Step 2

Highlight the topic and underline the controlling idea in each of the following topic sentences as shown in the examples. Think about the use of topic, controlling idea and topic sentence in writing a paragraph.

Examples:

Running provides many healthful benefits.

The basics of using an SLR camera can be mastered with considerable practice.

When writing a laboratory report, you must complete four sections.

1. Effective leadership requires specific qualities that anyone can develop.

2. People can avoid burglaries by taking certain precautions.

3. There are several advantages to grow up in a small town.

4. Most U. S. universities require a 100-point TOEFL score for a number of reasons.

5. Good manners are important in all countries, but ways of expressing good manners are different.

6. Pets are important to people because they can improve the overall health of the pet owner.

Step 3

Read the following topic sentences, and answer questions about these sentences.

1. Today I'm going to discuss the benefits of gardening.

2. Pets are important to people because they can improve the overall health of the pet owner.

3. The United States suffered a lot during the Civil War.

4. Sherman's destruction in the South during the Civil War also caused incredible suffering.

5. Christmas trees are either cedars or firs.

6. All dogs need food.

7. All dogs need regular care, including healthy food, and children are the best ones to do it.

8. Although gardening has many health benefits, people still have to be cautious when outside.

9. To improve proficiency, one needs to acquire some skills.

10. They moved to a new apartment last month.

Questions:

1. Is the topic and controlling idea clearly stated in each topic sentence?

2. Is the controlling idea in each topic sentence well balanced?

3. What is the difference between No. 3 and No. 4, and between No. 6 and No. 7?

4. Does each topic sentence express an idea to be developed or supported afterwards?

5. What problems can be found in those bad topic sentences? Make a list of the problems.

6. Apart from stating the topic and the controlling idea, what do you think a good topic sentence should be like?

Then work in groups and summarize what a good topic sentence(TS) should be like.

1. A good topic sentence should tell _____.

2. A topic sentence should not only tell _____.

3. The topic introduced in a TS should be _____.

4. The idea expressed in a TS should be _____.

5. The idea expressed in a TS should not be _____.

A good topic sentence:
- A complete sentence, grammatically correct
- The topic and the controlling idea clearly stated
- The controlling idea being well-balanced, allowing full development (Neither too general or vague nor too narrow or specific)
- Not an announcement of the topic
- Not a statement of fact or specific detail

ACTIVITY 2 ▶

Learning to write a good topic sentence

Step 1

Choose an appropriate topic sentence for each of the following paragraphs.

1. _____. North Americans send cards for many occasions. They send cards to family and friends on birthdays and holidays. They also send thank-you cards, get well cards, graduation cards, and congratulation cards. It is very common to buy cards in stores and send them through the mail, but turning on the computer and sending cards over the Internet is also popular.

   A. Sending cards is very popular in North America.

   B. Birthday cards are the most popular kind of card.

   C. It is important to send thank-you cards.

2. _____. I enjoy summer sports like water skiing and baseball. The weather is usually sunny and hot, so I can go to the beach almost every day. Gardening is my hobby and I spend many summer days working in my garden. Unfortunately, the days pass too quickly in summer.

   A. I like to garden in summer.

   B. Summer is my favorite season.

   C. Summer is too short.

3. _____. First of all, we need money to repair old roads and build new roads. We also need more to pay teachers' salaries and to pay for services such as trash collection. Finally, more tax money is needed to give financial help to the poor citizens of the city. It is clear that the city will have serious problems if taxes are not raised soon.

   A. We should raise city taxes.

   B. City taxes are too high.

   C. City taxes pay for new roads.

4. _____. For example, a person can have breakfast in New York, board an airplane, and have dinner in Paris. A businesswoman in London can instantly place an order with a factory in Hong Kong by sending a fax. Furthermore, a schoolboy in Tokyo can turn on a TV and watch a baseball game being played in Los Angeles.

A. Airplanes have changed our lives.

B. Advances in technology have made the world seem smaller.

C. The fax machine was an important invention.

5. _____. One thing you must consider is the quality of the university's educational program. You also need to think about the school's size and location. Finally, you must be sure to consider the university's tuition to make sure you can afford going to school there.

A. It is expensive to attend a university in the United States.

B. There are several factors to consider when you choose a university to attend.

C. You should consider getting a good education.

Step 2

Write a topic sentence for each of the following paragraphs.

1. Some people walk on a treadmill at home or ride a bicycle. Others like to go out dancing, do aerobics, or work out in a gym. Some other people prefer to swim.

   _____.

2. My parents have gone out for the evening. Just as I settle down to read or watch TV, my little brother demands that I play with him. If I get a telephone call, he screams or knocks something over. I always have to hang up to find out what's wrong with him. He refuses to let me eat a snack in peace. Usually he wants half of whatever I have to eat. Then when he finally grows tired, it takes about an hour for him to fall asleep. _____

   _____.

3. _____. Both are bodies of water, but oceans are very large bodies of salt water, while lakes are much smaller bodies of fresh water.

Lakes are usually surrounded by land, while oceans are what surround continents. Both have plants and animals living in them. The ocean is home to the largest animals on the planet, whereas lakes support much smaller forms of life. When it is time for a vacation, both will make a great place to visit and enjoy.

Step 3

Work in groups, choose a topic from the topics listed below, and practice writing a topic sentence for a paragraph, by following the steps suggested.

1. Making friends with strangers

2. Texting while driving

3. Purchasing a car or renting a car

4. Online meal ordering

5. My _____ Chinese festival

- **Follow these steps in your writing:**
(1) First, choose a topic you like.
(2) Think of an idea or opinion you want to express about the topic, as the controlling idea. Make sure that the controlling idea is neither too general nor too specific.
(3) Write a sentence, with your topic and controlling idea included.
(4) Improve the sentence to make it concise, emphatic and well-balanced, so that the paragraph to be written will be focused, well-organized and well-developed.

TASK TWO
Understanding Functions of Different Paragraphs

Step 1

Work in pairs, read the following passage, and underline the topic sentence in each paragraph. Then discuss questions about the paragraphs in this passage.

Friendship

1. A dictionary contains a definition of friendship somewhere in the F's between the words "fear" and "Friday." An encyclopedia supplies interesting facts on friendship. But all the definitions and facts do not convey what friendship is really all about. It cannot be understood through words or explanations. The only way to understand friendship is through experience. It is an experience that involves all the senses.

2. Friendship can be seen. It is seen in an old couple sitting in the park holding hands. It is the way they touch, a touch as light as a leaf floating in the autumn air, a touch so strong that years of living could not pull them apart. Friendship is seen in a child freely sharing the last cookie. It is the small arm over the shoulder of another as they walk on the playground. Seeing friendship is not casual. It is watching for subtlety, but friendship is there for eyes that can see.

3. Friendship can be heard. It is heard in the words of two friends who squeezed in lunch together on an extremely busy day. It is the way they talk to each other, not the words. Their tone is unique. Friendship can be heard by those willing to listen.

4. Friendship is felt in a touch. It is a pat on the back from a teammate, a high five between classes, the slimy, wet kiss from the family dog. It's a touch that reassures that someone is there, someone who cares. The touch communicates

more than words or gestures. It is instantly understood and speaks volumes beyond the point of contact, to the heart.

5. Friendship has a taste. It tastes like homemade bread, the ingredients all measured and planned, then carefully mixed and kneaded, then the quiet waiting as the dough rises. Hot from the oven, the bread tastes more than the sum of its ingredients. There is something else there, perhaps the thoughts of the baker as her hands knead the dough, or her patience as she waits for the dough to rise. Unseen and unmeasured, this is the ingredient that makes the difference. Warm, fresh from the oven with a little butter, the difference you taste is friendship.

6. Friendship has a smell. It smells like the slightly burnt cookies your brother made especially for you. It smells like your home when stepping into it after being away for a long time. It smells like a sandbox or a sweaty gym. Friendship has a variety of smells. Taken for granted at the moment, they define the memory of friendship.

7. Friendship, more than the other senses, is an experience of the heart. It is the language of the heart—a language without words, vowels, or consonants; a language that, whether seen, felt, heard, or tasted, is understood by the heart. Like air fills the lungs, friendship fills the heart, allowing us to experience the best life has to offer: a friend.

Questions:
1. What are the functions of paragraph 1, paragraphs 2-6 and paragraph 7 in the passage?
2. What is included in the underlined sentence in paragraph 1? What is the role of this underlined sentence in the whole passage?
3. What is the TS of each of paragraphs 2 — 6? What are the roles of these paragraphs?
4. Which aspect does each paragraph focus on?
5. What is the TS of paragraph 7? What is the role of this TS in the whole passage?

Step 2

Work in groups, and summarize the functions of different paragraphs in this passage.

1. Introductory paragraph: _____

2. Body paragraph: _____

3. Concluding paragraph: _____

Step 3

Choose a topic from the topics given in Step 3, Activity 2 of TASK ONE, and write topic sentences for different paragraphs about the topic you choose.

- Your topic: _____

- Your controlling idea: _____

  _____

- Sentence stating the topic, main idea (and big picture) of the whole passage in an introductory paragraph: _____

  _____

- Topic sentence(s) for body paragraph(s): _____

  _____

- Topic sentence for a concluding paragraph: _____

  _____

TASK THREE

Understanding Different Purposes of Paragraphs

ACTIVITY 1 ▶

Identifying purposes of writing different paragraphs

Step 1

Read the following paragraphs, and underline the topic sentence of each paragraph.

1. Sunset is the time of day when our sky meets the outer space solar winds. There are blue, pink, and purple swirls, spinning and twisting, like clouds of balloons caught in a blender. The sun moves slowly to hide behind the line of horizon, while the moon races to take its place in prominence atop the night sky. People slow to a crawl, entranced, fully forgetting the deeds that still must be done. There is a coolness, a calmness, when the sun does set.

2. On July 16, 1969, the Apollo 11 spacecraft launched from the Kennedy Space Center in Florida. Its mission was to go where no human being had gone before—the moon! The crew consisted of Neil Armstrong, Michael Collins, and Buzz Aldrin. The spacecraft landed on the moon in the Sea of Tranquility, a basaltic flood plain, on July 20, 1969. The moonwalk took place the following day. On July 21, 1969, at precisely 10:56 EDT, Commander Neil Armstrong emerged from the Lunar Module and took his famous first step onto the moon's surface. He declared, "That's one small step for man, one giant leap for mankind." It was a monumental moment in human history!

3. It was July 21, 1969, and Neil Armstrong awoke with a start. It was the day he would become the first human being to ever walk on the moon. The journey had begun several days earlier, when on July 16th, the Apollo 11 launched from Earth headed into outer space. On board with Neil Armstrong were Michael Collins and

Buzz Aldrin. The crew landed on the moon in the Sea of Tranquility a day before the actual walk. Upon Neil's first step onto the moon's surface, he declared, "That's one small step for man, one giant leap for mankind." It sure was!

4. The school fair is right around the corner, and tickets have just gone on sale. We are selling a limited number of tickets at a discount, so move fast and get yours while they are still available. This is going to be an event you will not want to miss! First of all, the school fair is a great value when compared with other forms of entertainment. Also, your ticket purchase will help our school, and when you help the school, it helps the entire community. But that's not all! Every ticket you purchase enters you in a drawing to win fabulous prizes. And don't forget, you will have mountains of fun because there are acres and acres of great rides, fun games, and entertaining attractions! Spend time with your family and friends at our school fair. Buy your tickets now!

5. The school fair is right around the corner, and tickets have just gone on sale. Even though you may be busy, you will still want to reserve just one day out of an entire year to relax and have fun with us. Even if you don't have much money, you don't have to worry. The school fair is a community event, and therefore prices are kept low. Perhaps, you are still not convinced. Maybe you feel you are too old for fairs, or you just don't like them. Well, that's what my grandfather thought, but he came to last year's school fair and had this to say about it: "I had the best time of my life!" While it's true you may be able to think of a reason not to come, I'm also sure you can think of several reasons why you must come. We look forward to seeing you at the school fair!

Step 2

Work in groups and answer the following questions about the paragraphs above.

1. What is the purpose of writing each paragraph?
   Paragraph 1: to describe
   Paragraph 2:
   Paragraph 3:
   Paragraph 4:
   Paragraph 5:

2. What is the topic sentence of each paragraph?

3. Can the purpose of writing of each paragraph be identified only from the topic sentence of the paragraph?

4. How should we write topic sentences for paragraphs with different purposes of writing?

ASSIGNMENTS

1. Summarize the 3 types of paragraphs of different functions.

(1)

(2)

(3)

2. Summarize the 4 types of paragraphs with different purposes of writing.

(1)

(2)

(3)

(4)

3. Read the topics given in Step 3, Activity 2 of TASK ONE and analyze the purpose of writing of the paragraph about each topic. Then practice writing a topic sentence for a paragraph about each topic.

Module 2 Writing a Narrative Paragraph

When finishing the learning of this module,

Goal 1   I will be able to identify narrative paragraphs.

Goal 2   I will understand features of narrative paragraphs.

Goal 3   I will be able to write a narrative paragraph.

Section 1   Writing a Good Paragraph (2)

TASK ONE

Identifying Narrative Paragraphs

ACTIVITY ▶

Identifying features of narrative paragraphs

Step 1

Read the following paragraphs, and answer questions about the paragraphs.

1. A Once in a Life Time Experience

The one day I spent in Morocco, Africa was an experience of a lifetime. When I finally reached Morocco and got off the bus, there were four little girls standing shoeless in the hot sun. After I swallowed my tears, I could not even try to picture this in Africa as it is not something you often see in the U. S. Meanwhile my tourist guide instructed me not to give them money as it encouraged the children to beg; however, I was wearing four silver bracelets. As I walked over to the girls, their eyes watched my every move. Then I kneeled down to their level while I gave each girl a bracelet. They stood there gleaming at me, for they were pleased. I felt completely in disbelief that this tiny gesture could mean so much. Though this experience was upsetting, and a huge culture shock, it will stay with me forever.

2. Pedaling on My Own

Learning how to ride a bike for the first time was a nerve racking independent moment. I was about five years old when my sister informed me that I was too old to still be riding a bike with training wheels. That was the time I decided not to depend on them anymore. Even though I had some doubt, my sister and I went outside and started to take the little wheels off my bike. After my bike went through the transformation, I was now ready for the big moment. With butterflies in my stomach, I slowly got on the bike, and with my shaky hands, I gripped the handles tightly. Meanwhile my sister was holding on to me to help keep my balance. I was so afraid that she would let go, yet I was determined to ride this bike on my own. Next, with a little push from her, I started to pedal. The faster my bike went, the faster my heart raced. Finally, I looked back nervously and noticed that my sister let go of my bike a long time ago. I was so excited that I accomplished freedom on my bike that I forgot to pedal. The next step I remember, I was lying on the ground, yet I did not care because of the adrenaline rush. I will never forget the exhilarating moment and growing up stage of riding a bike without training wheels.

3. My Experiences on a Hot Summer Day

It was the 22nd of June, perhaps the hottest day of the summer when the temperature had soared to 44 degrees. The sun was shining brightly from the early morning. The earth was hot like a baking oven. I had to go out in the scorching heat to call in a doctor as my mother was sick. The roads were deserted. Plants and trees had withered away. Hot wind was blowing. It had added to the intensity of the heat. Life seemed to have come to a complete standstill. Animals were panting for breath. Birds were silent. Since I could not get any scooter or taxi, I had to walk on foot a distance of two kilometers. When I came back home with the doctor, I was completely shattered and exhausted. I also had fever. The doctor said that it was a case of heat stroke. I remained in bed for a week. During my illness, I often thought of the poor laborers who had to work both in winter and summer. I wondered how they managed to bear the biting cold of winter and the scorching heat of summer.

4. When You Met an Old Friend

Meeting an old friend unexpectedly always gives a pleasant surprise. It brings back to one's mind sweet memories of early childhood and school-days. We become nostalgic. We enjoy remembering the pranks of our childhood. Only last Sunday, I had such a pleasant experience. I went to the railway station to receive my brother who was coming from Bengaluru. The train was late by half an hour. I was walking about at the platform. I saw a young man staring at me. It appeared that I had seen him somewhere. However, I could recall nothing. I abandoned the thought and continued walking. But the man was trying to recollect something. I looked at him closely. Suddenly I recollected that we were class fellows fifteen years back when my father was posted in Calcutta. He was Akshat. How much he had changed! I approached him and said hesitantly, "Akshat!" He said, "Alok!" And we embraced each other. We were very pleased at this unexpected meeting. We asked about each other's career, families, etc. We talked a lot. We remembered our old friends and teachers. We enjoyed remembering our mischiefs about the good old days. Both of us were so changed. He was now a major in the army and I was a school teacher.

Questions:

1. What is the purpose of writing each of these paragraphs?
2. What kinds of information should be included in a narrative paragraph?
3. What is the topic sentence (TS) of each paragraph? What are the topic and the controlling idea in each TS?
4. What is the relation between the TS and the story told in each paragraph?

Step 2

Read the four paragraphs again, and discuss the following questions in groups.

1. Which tenses are used in the story telling in each paragraph? Why?
2. In what order are the events and the sentences arranged in each paragraph? Why?
3. What kinds of words or expressions are used to link what happens in the stories? Highlight these words and expressions in the paragraphs.
4. How does each paragraph open and end? Why?

5. Apart from telling a story, what else are expressed in these paragraphs?

6. Go over the underlined words, phrases or sentences in each paragraph. What are the parts of speeches and elements of these words or phrases in each sentence?

7. Why are these underlined words, phrases, and sentences used in each paragraph?

8. What role(s) do the underlined sentences play in paragraph 3?

TASK TWO
Understanding Features of Narrative Paragraphs

Step 1

Work in groups of 3 or 4 and summarize the features of narrative paragraphs, based on your discussions done in TASK ONE.

1. Organization features:

    (1) Purpose of writing: _____

    (2) Content (or elements) : _____

    _____

    (3) Main idea: _____

    (4) Order of events: _____

2. Language features:

    (1) Tense(s) of verbs: _____

    (2) Words and expressions indicating time or sequence: _____

    _____

    _____

(3) Some commonly used transitional expressions：

after, finally, soon, as (soon as), later, then, before, meanwhile, upon,
during, next, when, first, now, and while, etc.

(4) Descriptive language：

Types of words and expressions：*adj. adv. prepositional phrase, clauses, etc.*

Elements of these words or expressions in the sentences：_____

_____

TASK THREE
Writing a Narrative Paragraph

ACTIVITY 1 ▶

Narrating things happening over time

Step 1

Work in pairs and fill in the following blanks with correct prepositions and verbs in proper forms to form a paragraph.

Yesterday evening Jack (1) _____ (get) home (2) _____ (preposition) half past five. He immediately (3) _____ (make) himself a cup (4) _____ (preposition) coffee and (5) _____ (sit down) to read a book. He (6) _____ (read) the book (7) _____ (preposition) half past seven. Then, he (8) _____ (make) dinner and (9) _____ (get ready) to go out with his friends. When his friends (10) _____ (arrive), they (11) _____ (decide) to go out to see a film. He (12) _____ (stay out) until midnight with his friends. Finally, he (13) _____ (fall) asleep (14) _____ (preposition) about one o'clock.

ACTIVITY 2 ▶

Adding transition words and phrases

Step 1

Fill in blanks in this paragraph with appropriate transitions.

_____ I drove my rusty old car to visit my best friend. _____ I arrived, he had done his best to prepare a tasty meal. _____, we took a long walk through the park next to his home. _____ we had been out for more than an hour, my friend asked me if I could keep a secret. _____, I swore not to tell anyone anything. _____ he recounted a wild tale of a crazy night out on the town _____. _____, he told me he had met the woman of his dreams and that they were to get married _____. Imagine my surprise!

ACTIVITY 3 ▶

Adding adverbial clauses of time correctly

Step 1

Read the following two sentences with time clauses and find out the difference(s) in the use of time clauses in the sentences and the expected effects.

1. After we had finished our homework, we watched a funny movie.
2. They attended a meeting as soon as they arrived in Chicago.
   - The difference(s):

   - The effects of the difference(s):

Step 2

Rewrite the two sentences above, by changing the positions of the time clauses and using comma correctly.

1. _____

2. _____

ACTIVITY 4 ▶

Using descriptive language

Step 1

Rewrite the sentences below, using descriptive language to spice up the writing.

1. After that, the man went home.

   _____

2. Later, we drove to a restaurant.

   _____

3. He had finished the report before I gave the presentation.

   _____

4. The children attended the class.

   _____

5. My friends asked for help.

   _____

ASSIGNMENTS

Practice writing a narrative paragraph on one of the following topics.

1. The happiest moment in my life
2. My first experience in...
3. Learning to swim / play the guitar /...
4. Using smart phones

Follow the steps listed below in your paragraph writing.

1. Choose a topic, narrow down and write down your specific topic.
2. Think of a story or event which is related to the topic.
3. Decide on a point or an idea you want to express through the story telling, or a lesson or moral you have learned from the story.
4. Write your topic sentence, with the topic and the controlling idea included.
5. Decide on the position of the topic sentence.
6. Arrange the developing sentences in time order, and use verbs in proper tenses in your writing.
7. Use transition words, phrases or clauses properly to indicate time or sequence.
8. Use proper descriptive language to make your writing vivid and interesting.

Module 3　Writing a Descriptive Paragraph

When finishing the learning of this module,

Goal 1　I will be able to identify descriptive paragraphs.

Goal 2　I will understand features of descriptive paragraphs.

Goal 3　I will be able to write a descriptive paragraph.

Section 1　Writing a Good Paragraph (2)

TASK ONE

Identifying Descriptive Paragraphs

Step 1

Read the following paragraph, and answer the questions.

Sunset is the time of day when our sky meets the outer space solar winds. There are blue, pink, and purple swirls, spinning and twisting, like clouds of balloons caught in a blender. The sun moves slowly to hide behind the line of horizon, while the moon rises to take its place in prominence atop the night sky. People slow to a crawl, entranced, fully forgetting the deeds that still must be done. There is a coolness, a calmness, when the sun does set.

Questions:

1. What is the purpose of writing this paragraph?
2. What are the topic and the main idea of this paragraph?
3. What specific details are provided to support the topic and the main idea?

4. What is expressed at the end of this paragraph?

Step 2

Work in pairs and summarize what a descriptive paragraph should be like.

A descriptive paragraph _____

_____

_____

TASK TWO

Understanding Features of Descriptive Paragraphs

ACTIVITY 1 ▶

Analyzing descriptive paragraphs

Step 1

Work in groups. Read the following paragraphs carefully and answer questions after each paragraph.

1. The Blond Guitar

My most valuable possession is an old, slightly warped blond guitar — the first instrument I taught myself how to play. It's nothing fancy, just a Madeira folk guitar, all scuffed and scratched and fingerprinted. At the top is a bramble of copper-wound strings, each one hooked through the eye of a silver tuning key. The strings are stretched down a long, slim neck, its frets tarnished, the wood worn by years of fingers pressing chords and picking notes. *The body of the Madeira is shaped like an enormous yellow pear*, one that was slightly damaged in shipping. The blond wood has been chipped and gouged to gray, particularly where the pick guard fell off years ago. No, it's not a beautiful instrument, but it still lets me make music, and for that I will always treasure it.

—by Jeremy Burden

Questions：

1. What are expressed in the topic sentence and the concluding sentence?
2. Which parts of the guitar are described and in what order? Why?
3. What specific details are described about each part? Why are these details described?
4. What sense(s) does the writer mainly appeal to in the writing of this paragraph?
5. Apart from the appearance, what else is expressed about the guitar?
6. What is the use of the underlined adjectives in the description?
7. Which rhetorical device (修辞手法) is used in the *italicized part*(斜体部分), and for what purpose?

2. Gregory

Gregory is my beautiful gray Persian cat. He walks with pride and grace, performing a dance of disdain as he slowly lifts and lowers each paw with the delicacy of a ballet dancer. His pride, however, does not extend to his appearance, for he spends most of his time indoors watching television and growing fat. He enjoys TV commercials, especially those for Meow Mix and 9 Lives. His familiarity with cat food commercials has led him to reject generic brands of cat food in favor of only the most expensive brands. Gregory is as finicky about visitors as he is about what he eats, befriending some and repelling others. He may snuggle up against your ankle, begging to be petted, or he may imitate a skunk and stain your favorite trousers. Gregory does not do this to establish his territory, as many cat experts think, but to humiliate me because he is jealous of my friends. After my guests have fled, I look at the old fleabag snoozing and smiling to himself in front of the television set, and I have to forgive him for his obnoxious, but endearing habits.

—by Barbara Carter

Questions：

1. How does this paragraph open and end?
2. What does the writer describe about the cat?
3. What specific details are described about the behavior of the cat? Give examples.

4. What kinds of feelings toward the cat is expressed in this paragraph? Give examples.

5. What rhetorical device is used in the description of the cat, and for what purpose?

3. Inside District School #7, Niagara County, New York

Inside, the school <u>smelled</u> smartly of varnish and wood smoke from the potbellied stove. On gloomy days, not unknown in upstate New York in this region south of Lake Ontario and east of Lake Erie, the windows emitted a vague, gauzy light, not much reinforced by ceiling lights. We squinted at the blackboard, that seemed far away since it was on a small platform, where Mrs. Dietz's desk was also positioned, at the front, left of the room. We sat in rows of seats, smallest at the front, largest at the rear, attached at their bases by metal runners, like a toboggan; the wood of these desks seemed beautiful to me, smooth and of the red-burnished hue of horse chestnuts. The floor was bare wooden planks. An American flag hung limply at the far left of the blackboard and above the blackboard, and running across the front of the room, designed to draw our eyes to it avidly, worshipfully, were paper squares showing that beautifully shaped script known as Parker Penmanship.

—by Joyce Carol Oates

Questions:

1. What sense does the writer appeal to at the beginning of the description?

2. What does the writer describe about the classroom? In what order?

3. What specific details are described about the things mentioned in the classroom?

4. Why are these very specific details described?

5. Underline descriptive adjectives and adverbs in the paragraph.

ACTIVITY 2 ▶

Summarizing features of descriptive paragraphs

Step 1

Work in groups of 3 or 4 and summarize features of descriptive paragraphs, based on your discussion in Activity 1.

1. Organization features:

   (1) Purpose of writing: _____

   (2) Topic: _____

   (3) Supporting details: _____

   (4) Main idea: _____

   (5) Order of description: _____

2. Language features:

   (1) Using descriptive language:

   - Types of words and expressions: adjective, adverb, prepositional phrase, gerund, etc.
   - Elements in a sentence: _____

   _____

   (2) Appealing to the five senses: sight, _____, _____, _____, _____

   (3) Rhetorical devices: _____

   _____

TASK THREE
Writing a Descriptive Paragraph

ACTIVITY 1 ▶

Understanding ways of description

Step 1

Work in groups. Read the following descriptive paragraph, and find the sentences providing descriptive details in the ways listed below. Write the numbers of the sentences in the blanks provided.

(1) Natasha's basement was our sanctuary. (2) I return to it in my best dreams and wake up feeling like I could die happy. (3) Even today I could paint a perfect picture of it, right up to the last piece of neglected pizza crust festering under the ping-pong table. (4) The spilled root beer and duck sauce shining over the nappy brown carpet indicated nights of giggles and prank calls, times when we were far too occupied to consider the absurd possibility of cleaning up. (5) Popcorn got crushed into the carpet and was never quite cleaned up. (6) You could smell this mixture of sweetness and butter even when you stood on the front porch. (7) Nothing ever got erased, either. (8) It was like memory. (9) With enough time and will power, you could find almost anything down there. (10) Katie had once recovered her third grade Tamagotchi from the storage closet. (11) Another time, Nora had unearthed a disposable camera with undeveloped pictures I had taken during our fourth grade trip to Ellis Island. (12) The television in the basement was always on, but no one ever seemed to watch it. (13) We were too busy laughing over our latest stupid game of Rummikub, prank calling our crushes, or listening for the doorbell that told us the pizza was here. (14) The silver Christmas garland around the banisters was pretty much a permanent fixture; the same birthday steamers celebrated three shoe-sizes of birthdays, eventually lost their color, and seemed to peel off the walls on their own accord. (15) As it was, with a net-less ping-pong table and a set of bare mattresses facing the TV, the

basement looked more like the Fiona Apple "Criminal" video than a place to raise your children. (16) And that was exactly why three extra toothbrushes made their way to the downstairs bathroom. (17) All of us could have lived and died there.

1. Sentences <u>(1)—(2)</u> introduce the subject that is being described, Natasha's basement, and make it clear that this place is very important to the writer.
2. Sentences ＿＿＿—＿＿＿ use descriptive adjective(s) and specific, definitive examples to express the importance of the place and sentence 8 uses rhetorical device (simile) to add deep meaning.
3. Sentences ＿＿＿—＿＿＿ appeal to the readers' sense of taste and smell, and use descriptive adjectives to provide a specific experience for the reader.
4. Sentence ＿＿＿—＿＿＿ uses simile to compare the basement to a notorious music video, adding an extra layer of meaning, making the description more appealing.
5. Sentences ＿＿＿—＿＿＿ appeal to the sense of sound and use the sounds in the basement to help give a sense of what it was like to actually be there.
6. Sentence ＿＿＿—＿＿＿ appeals to the sense of sight and uses descriptive adjectives to create a visual picture of some things in the basement: old pizza crust and a ping-pong table.
7. Sentence ＿＿(14)＿＿ describes some specific items which are special and unusual, making the description unique and interesting.
8. Sentences (16)—(17) end the paragraph by reminding readers of what is described and leave a lasting idea of the place in the readers' minds.

ACTIVITY 2 ▶

Describing things in proper order

Step 1

Work in pairs. Rearrange the order of the following sentences to make the description logical and coherent.

A Friendly Clown

A. The blue eyes are outlined in black with thin, dark lashes flowing from the brows.

B. On one corner of my dresser sits a smiling toy clown on a tiny unicycle—a gift I received last Christmas from a close friend.

C. The clown wears a fluffy, two-tone nylon costume.

D. The clown's short yellow hair, made of yarn, covers its ears but is parted above the eyes.

E. Surrounding its ankles and disguising its long black shoes are big pink bows.

F. The left side of the outfit is light blue, and the right side is red.

G. The two colors merge in a dark line that runs down the center of the small outfit.

H. The white spokes on the wheels of the unicycle gather in the center and expand to the black tire so that the wheel somewhat resembles the inner half of a grapefruit.

I. It has cherry-red cheeks, nose, and lips, and its broad grin disappears into the wide, white ruffle around its neck.

J. As a cherished gift from my good friend Tran, this colorful figure greets me with a smile every time I enter my room.

K. The clown and unicycle together stand about a foot high.

Your answer: _____

ACTIVITY 3 ▶

Using descriptive words and phrases

Step 1

Work in pairs. Fill in blanks in the following paragraph with appropriate words or phrases from the box below to make the paragraph vivid and complete.

cooler	tired	special atmosphere
aroma	green	bigger
quick	friendly	important

Cafes are essential places for students and teachers who want to have a break. Although they are just small shops, they have a (1) _____. You can smell the (2) _____ of coffee and they are often located in a (3) _____ part of the university surrounded by trees. The best cafes are air-conditioned inside but they have a deck outside which is where (4) _____ groups like to hang out and chat. Inside where it is (5) _____ other students read books, work on computers or check their messages on their smart phones. The service is usually (6) _____ and (7) _____. Moreover, if you are (8) _____ from studying, you can usually find a café wherever you are in the university. The cafés are not just shops; they are an (9) _____ part of university culture.

ASSIGNMENTS

Practice writing a descriptive paragraph by following the steps listed below.

1. **Choose an appropriate topic about**
   - a specific person, object or place that you know well.
   - something that has special meaning to you.

2. **Brain storm on the topic, and study the topic closely by**
   - appealing to the five senses: sight, sound, smell, taste, and feeling.
   - thinking of your own memories of or associations with the thing described.
   - thinking of your goal of description and the message to convey through your description.
   - selecting details related to the topic and best help express your ideas or feelings.

3. **Write the descriptive paragraph by**
   - opening with a topic sentence (TS) stating the topic and its significance or special meaning.
   - adding developing sentences to give a focused and detail-rich account of the thing described.
   - arranging the details in a logical order, and using transitions properly.
   - appealing to the five senses in providing descriptive details.
   - using descriptive adjectives and rhetorical devices to make the description vivid.
   - concluding with a sentence that circles back to the idea expressed in the TS.

Module 4 Writing an Expository Paragraph—Interpretation

When finishing the learning of this module,

Goal 1   I will be able to identify features of expository paragraphs.

Goal 2   I will understand the ways of interpretation in organizing expository paragraphs.

Goal 3   I will know language features in paragraphs of interpretation.

Goal 4   I will be able to write expository paragraphs of interpretation.

Section 1   Writing a Good Paragraph (2)

TASK ONE

Identifying Expository Paragraphs

Step 1

Work in pairs. Read the following paragraphs, and answer questions after your reading.

1. Dinosaurs existed about 250 million years ago to 65 million years ago. This era is broken up into three periods known as the Triassic, Jurassic and Cretaceous periods. The Triassic Period lasted for 35 million years from 250 to 205 million years ago. Planet Earth was a very different place back then. All the continents were united to form one huge land mass known as Pangaea. The Jurassic Period was the second phase. The continents began shifting apart. The time scale for this famous period is from 205 to 138 million years ago. The Cretaceous Period was the last period of the dinosaurs. It spanned a time from 138 million to about 65 million years ago. In this period the continents fully separated. However, Australia and Antarctica were still united.

2. Smoking is bad for your health. Smoking harms nearly every organ of the body. Cigarette smoking causes 87 percent of lung cancer deaths. It is also responsible for many other cancers and health problems. These include lung disease, heart and blood vessel disease, stroke and cataracts. Women who smoke have a greater chance of certain pregnancy problems or having a baby die from sudden infant death syndrome (SIDS). Your smoke is also bad for other people—they breathe in your smoke secondhand and can get many of the same problems as smokers do.

3. Now TV has become necessary in our life. We can get all kinds of information through TV such as the weather, information, or laws, knowledge and so on. We can watch some funny programs to relax and make us happy. The distance between countries is shortened with the help of TV. We can get to know all kinds of events around the world. Though TV is good for us, sometimes it has bad influence. Some students spend so much free time in watching TV that they have no time to study. It influences their lessons. And some programs are not good for children. As far as I'm concerned, we should choose proper programs at proper time for people in different ages, especially for children. We can have entertainment and learning combination.

Questions:
1. What is the purpose of writing each paragraph?
2. Is there a topic sentence(TS) in each paragraph? Underline it. If not, what TS is implied in the paragraph?
3. What are the topic and the main idea of each paragraph?
4. Does the TS of each paragraph state a fact or express an opinion? Give your reasons.
5. What kinds of specific details are provided to support the TS in each paragraph?
6. How are the developing sentences organized in each paragraph?
7. Is the writer objective or subjective in writing each paragraph? Give your reasons.
8. Are there many descriptive adjectives or adverbs used in each paragraph? Why or why not?
9. How is each paragraph concluded?

Step 2

Work in groups of 3 to 4. Discuss and summarize the features of expository paragraphs.

1. Purpose of writing: _____

2. Topic: _____

3. Controlling idea: _____

4. Supporting details: _____

5. Concluding sentence: _____

6. General tone of writing: _____

Step 3

Explain in your own words what an expository paragraph is.

An expository paragraph _____

_____

TASK TWO

Understanding the Ways of Interpretation

ACTIVITY 1 ▶

Analyzing the ways of organization

Work in groups. Read the paragraphs in TASK ONE again, analyze the content and the organization of the paragraphs and fill information in the following diagram.

Para.	Topic	Controlling idea	Supporting details
1			**Detailed information:** time scale of each period and the details about the Planet Earth
2	Smoking	bad for health	**Bad effects:** lung cancer, health problems, lung, heart, blood vessel diseases, etc.
3			**Advantages and disadvantages:**

An expository paragraph aims to inform readers of certain kind of information. It can be organized in different ways, according to the logical relation between the idea expressed and the supporting details provided.

Ways to organize expository paragraphs (1)

1. Interpretation: explaining or introducing in one of the following 3 ways
   - **Interpretation — Topic pattern**
     To explain about a certain topic with specific information or details
   - **Interpretation — Cause or effect**
     To explain a causal relation with focus on either the cause or the effect
   - **Interpretation — Advantage and/or disadvantage**
     To support the main idea by explaining advantages and/or disadvantages

ACTIVITY 2 ▶

Identifying the ways of organization adopted

Step 1

Work in pairs. Read the information box above and identify the topic, the main idea and the way of interpretation adopted in each of the following paragraphs.

4. Nowadays, our daily life is filled with advertisements. We can see a variety of advertising everywhere. Those advertisings affect our consumption behavior. As a popular saying goes "everything has its two sides", ads are no exception. For us consumers, advertisings can not only help us easily find out things that we truly need, but also can help us compare prices when they are listed in ads. What's more, some ads are very foresighted, which can help us broaden our vision. For a company, interesting ads can draw consumers' attention, making consumers remember the products. Also, good ads can deliver the culture of the company. However, ads also have disadvantages. Some ads can give false or misleading information to consumers, especially to teenagers. Some people may lose their individuality because of the ads. More importantly, some ads make the product looks good, but is not always true. Besides, ads will make the products' cost increase. This charge will be passed on to consumers.

   Topic: _____

   Main idea: _____

   Way of interpretation: _____

5. At the University of Bridgeport, student involvement and leadership in extracurricular activities is encouraged and celebrated. The Office of Campus Activities and Civic Engagement serves to advise and assist students with their programming efforts, provide training and leadership development, and coordinates local volunteer and community service opportunities for students. Over 50 registered clubs and organizations provide you with numerous

opportunities to participate in social, educational and cultural activities. The Office also publishes weekly and monthly activity calendars to keep the campus community updated on student events.

Topic: _____

Main idea: _____

Way of interpretation: _____

6. As we all know, reading books, especially the classical, make us better men day by day. Nevertheless, people, especially the young, seem to have stored those classical books merely on the shelf for an unbelievably long time, which can be attributed to various factors. On the one hand, modern people have to cope with the quick pace and unavoidable stress of their work or life; therefore, they can hardly devote time to reading books. On the other hand, people tend to be more material-oriented involving their social status, amount of wealth or prospects of getting promotion, which eclipse the important benefits from reading classical books.

Topic: _____

Main idea: _____

Way of interpretation: _____

TASK THREE
Understanding Language Features

ACTIVITY 1 ▶

Analyzing and identifying language features

Step 1

Work in groups. Read the 6 paragraphs in TASK ONE and TASK TWO, and find out the words or expressions as required below.

1. Find in paragraphs 2 and 6 words or expressions used to indicate causal relations or effects.

   (1) Smoking *is bad for* ...

   (2) Smoking *harms* ...

   (3) ... *causes* ... lung cancer deaths

   (4) _____

   (5) _____

   (6) _____

   (7) _____

   (8) _____

   (9) ... , which can be attributed to various factors.

2. Find in paragraphs 3 and 4 sentences indicating change of topic from advantages to disadvantages.

   _____

3. Find in paragraph 1 expressions used to introduce time of different period.

   (1) The Triassic Period lasted for... from... years ago

(2) _____

(3) _____

4. Find in paragraph 5 words or expressions with similar meaning as the word "help".

(1) _____

(2) _____

(3) _____

5. Underline transition words or phrases used in each paragraph, and find out the logical relations these transitions convey in the contexts.

Step 2

Work in groups and try to list more words or expressions commonly used to:

1. Explain cause or reason: _____

_____

_____

2. Explain result or effect: _____

_____

_____

3. Introduce an opposite point: _____

_____

_____

TASK FOUR
Writing an Interpretation Paragraph

Step 1

Practice writing an expository paragraph in 80 – 100 words, using one way of interpretation (topic pattern, cause or effect, advantage and/or disadvantage) in your writing.

Follow the steps listed below when writing your paragraph of Interpretation.

1. Choose one of the topics given below to write a paragraph.
   - Using mobile phones
   - Shopping online
   - Internet addiction
   - The city of Xi'an/Tianjin/Suzhou/Hangzhou/...
   - The development of computer
2. Narrow down to a specific topic and brainstorm on the topic.
3. Decide on the way of interpretation to be used in your writing.
4. Choose relevant supporting details.
5. Write a topic sentence with your topic and controlling idea stated.
6. Write developing sentences with supporting details, including major developing sentences and minor developing sentences.
7. Arrange the sentences in proper order, according to the way of interpretation you choose to use in this paragraph writing.
8. Use appropriate words or expressions to help interpret details or the main idea, or to express logical relations like cause or effect, advantage and/or disadvantage, etc.
9. Use transition words or expressions to make the paragraph logical and coherent.
10. Write a concluding sentence to close the paragraph properly.

ASSIGNMENTS

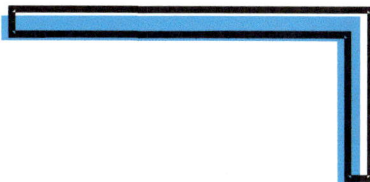

Write two expository paragraphs on the topics given in Step 1 of TASK FOUR, using the other two ways of interpretation that you didn't use in your writing in class. Follow the steps listed in TASK FOUR when you write the two paragraphs.

Module 5 Writing an Expository Paragraph—Classification and Extended-Definition

When finishing the learning of this module,

Goal 1　I will understand classification and extended-definition in organizing paragraphs.

Goal 2　I will know language features in paragraphs of classification and extended-definition.

Goal 3　I will be able to write paragraphs of classification and extended-definition.

Section 1　Writing a Good Paragraph (2)

TASK ONE

Understanding Ways of Organization

ACTIVITY 1 ▶

Identifying paragraphs of classification

Step 1

Work in pairs. Read the following paragraphs, and answer questions after your reading.

1. Shoppers can be classified according to their shopping techniques, as necessity shoppers, over spenders, and impulsive shoppers. Necessity shoppers have an uncomplicated and normal shopping technique. They purchase only the items that are necessary, such as food and toiletries, and they only get these items when they need them. The over spenders purchase too many items and they

spend too much money on them. They buy unnecessary products, such as clothes and accessories. They can turn a simple trip to the store into a wallet draining extravaganza. Finally, there are impulsive shoppers. They are a combination between necessity shoppers and over spenders. They intend to be necessity shoppers by buying items that they need, but they turn into over spenders by buying unnecessary clothes and useless items. Even though there are millions of shoppers worldwide, they can easily be classified into these three types of shoppers.

2. Music is often divided into four categories according to its origins and instruments: classical music, traditional music, rock music, and jazz music. The first kind, classical music, originated in Europe a few hundred years ago. Most of the original classical music was composed in Italy, Germany, Austria and Russia. It is usually played by a variety of string instruments and wind instruments. The second type of music is traditional music. It is the music that comes from a particular culture. Each culture has its own traditional music that is played by special instruments. Another kind of music is rock music. It probably began in Europe about 30 or 40 years ago. Rock is generally a loud kind of music, played with a strong beat. Rock musicians often use electric instruments, such as electric guitars and electric pianos, but other instruments can also be used. The fourth kind of music is jazz. It probably comes from African originally. Jazz has a different kind of rhythm from other kinds of music. A variety of musical instruments are used to play this kind of music, especially wind instruments.

Questions:
1. What is the purpose of writing each paragraph?
2. Is there a topic sentence(TS) in each paragraph? What is the topic? What is the main idea?
3. What kinds of specific details are provided to support the TS in each paragraph?
4. How are the developing sentences organized in each paragraph? In which order are the different types of shoppers/music mentioned?
5. How is each paragraph concluded?

ACTIVITY 2 ▶

Identifying paragraphs of extended-definition

Step 1

Work in pairs. Read the following paragraphs, and answer questions after your reading.

3. Friendship is the relationship between persons who can help each other in need and who have much in common. Friendship can make people happy and successful. In my opinion, friendship is one of the most precious things we have for several reasons. First, we can lead a happy life if we have some friends to share feelings, for joy that is shared will be doubled and sorrow shared will be reduced. For instance, I felt a little lonely during my first days after I came to college because it was my first time to be away from my family and away from my old friends.

4. Immobilization can range from total inaction to mild indecision and hesitancy. Does your anger keep you from saying, feeling, or doing something? If so, then you are immobilized. Does your shyness prevent you from meeting people you want to know? If so, you are immobilized and missing out on experiences that are rightfully yours. Is your hate and jealousy helping you to grow an ulcer or to raise your blood pressure? Does it keep you from working effectively on the job? Are you unable to sleep because of a negative present-moment feeling? These are all signs of immobilization. Immobilization: A state, however mild or serious, in which you are not functioning at the level that you would like to. If feelings lead to such a state, you need to look no further for a reason to get rid of them.

Questions:

1. What is the purpose of writing each paragraph?
2. Is there a topic sentence(TS) in each paragraph? What are the topic and the main idea of each paragraph?
3. What kinds of specific details are provided to support the TS in each paragraph?
4. How are the developing sentences organized in each paragraph?
5. How is each paragraph concluded?

RESULTS of your discussion:

Ways to organize expository paragraphs (2)

Apart from ways of interpretation (topic pattern, cause or effect, advantage and/or disadvantage), there are also other ways of organization commonly adopted in expository paragraph writing.

- **Classification**

A paragraph of classification begins with a topic sentence that divides a subject into several categories. The other sentences clarify similarities and differences in different categories.

- **Extended-definition**

An extended-definition paragraph informs by explaining and clarifying something complex. It not only gives a definition but also provides an expanded analysis and illustration of a complex concept that may be abstract, controversial, unfamiliar, or frequently misunderstood. It is an in-depth explanation which may include examples or comparison.

ACTIVITY 3 ▶

Identifying the ways of organization adopted

Step 1

Work in groups of 3 or 4. Read the information box above and identify the topic, the main idea and the way of organization adopted in each of the following paragraphs.

5. Friends can be classified according to their honesty, loyalty, the type that fits you into their schedule, or the type that finds time for you when they need something. An honest friend tells you the truth even if it's not always what you want to hear. In the long run, that honest friend may have saved you from embarrassment or possibly rejection. They give you constructive criticism overall. The loyal friend is the type of friend that will be there for you through the thick and the thin. They don't care how good or bad you may look one day; they are sensitive to your feelings, they respect you and the other people in your life, and most of all they will never let you down when times are hard. They may be what you call a best friend. The third group, the person that fits you into their schedule, is the type of person that is always on the go. They barely have time for themselves let alone another person. More than likely they will not be there for you when you need them most, because they are so wrapped up in their busy, hectic life. Then you have the self-absorbent type of "friend" that finds time for you only when they need something. This type of person isn't what you would call a friend. This person may always be extremely nice to you because they know that if they are nice to you then they will more than likely get what they want. They will call you every once in a while when it is almost time for them to use that person again. It may be for a ride to work, home, or they just want somebody to hang out with because they have no other friends. If the person that is being used is smart they will eventually realize that they are getting used and will stop being there for that person.

Topic: _____

Main idea: _____

Way of organization: _____

6. A racist refers to someone who doesn't accept other people for who they are, but rather pre-judges them based on their appearance or their skin color. The vast diversity of society makes it nearly impossible to eliminate all racial

tension. A racist usually has no other reason to hate somebody except for the fact that the other person may look different or have a different skin color than them. In the long run, racists are only hurting themselves because they are limiting their knowledge of different cultures and people and they are not broadening their horizons. Racists are extremely closed minded individuals and they strictly adhere to their own set of beliefs and morals without any regard for other people's belief systems. Racists are too selfish and not open minded enough to accept people for the way they are.

Topic: _____

Main idea: _____

Way of organization: _____

TASK TWO

Understanding the Language Features

ACTIVITY ▶

Analyzing and identifying language features

Step 1

Work in groups. Read the 6 paragraphs in TASK ONE, and find out the words or expressions as required below.

1. Find in paragraphs 1, 2 and 5 sentences which express classification of categories:

   Paragraph 1: Shoppers can be classified according to their shopping techniques, as necessity shoppers, over spenders, and impulsive shoppers.

   Paragraph 2: _____

   _____

Paragraph 5: _____

_____

2. Find out words or expressions in paragraphs 1, 2 and 5 to list different types:

Paragraph 1: Necessity shoppers...

The over spenders...

Finally, there are impulsive shoppers.

Paragraph 2: The first kind, classical music,... _____

_____

_____

The fourth kind of music is jazz.

Paragraph 5: An honest friend tells you...

_____

_____

Then you have the self-absorbent type of "friend" that...

3. Find in paragraph 1 adjectives used to describe different kinds of shoppers:

Necessity shoppers: uncomplicated, normal, _____

Over spender: _____

Impulsive shoppers: _____

4. Find in paragraph 2 expressions to explain the origin of a certain kind of music:

originated in, _____

5. Find in paragraph 5 specific things a certain type of friend usually does:

Honest friend: tells you the truth _____

_____

Loyal friend: _____

_____

The person that fits you into their schedule: _____

_____

_____

The self-absorbent type of "friend": They may be nice to you in order to get what they want. They will call you when they want to use that person.

6. Find in paragraphs 3, 4 and 6 sentences giving definitions of the concepts explained.

Paragraph 3: _____

Paragraph 4: _____

Paragraph 6: A racist refers to someone who ... _____

7. Based on the sentences you find to give definitions, summarize the ways of giving definitions by filling blanks with the choices given below.

A term *is/refers to/can be defined as* _____ that/who _____.

A. a general term   B. description of specific features

8. Underline the transition words or phrases used in each paragraph, and find out the logical relations they convey in the contexts.

Useful expressions for paragraph writing

• **Classification**

　　... can be divided / classified / categorized ...

　　... include / consist of / fall into ...

　　... be made up of / be composed of ...

　　the first type / the second kind / the last category

• **Extended-definition**

　　... is / means / refers to ... / can be defined as ... / is known as ...

　　By ... , we mean ... ; By ... , ... is meant.

　　... is called / is referred to as ...

（Use different expressions to avoid monotony in writing.）

TASK THREE
Writing A Classification Paragraph

Step 1

Practice writing a paragraph of classification in 80 – 100 words.

Follow the steps listed below when writing your paragraph of classification.

1. Choose one of the topics given below, and write a paragraph of classification.
   - Classmates
   - Teachers
   - Television programs
   - Movie endings
   - Sports fans
2. Narrow the topic down and brainstorm on the topic.
3. Decide on the way of classification in your writing.
4. Choose relevant supporting details for each type.
5. Write a topic sentence stating your topic and controlling idea (classification, type...).
6. Write developing sentences with enough specific details about each type.
7. Explain different types in the same order as they are mentioned in the topic sentence.
8. Use transition words or expressions in connecting the sentences.
9. Notice sentence variety in your writing.

ASSIGNMENTS

Choose 2 topics from the topics given below and practice writing 2 paragraphs of extended-definition. Follow the steps listed in TASK THREE, and give clear definitions and detailed explanations about each topic.

- Trust
- Kindness
- Sportsmanship
- A good parent
- Sense of humor

Module 6 Writing an Expository Paragraph—Process

When finishing the learning of this module,

Goal 1   I will understand the way of process in paragraph organization.

Goal 2   I will know language features in expository paragraphs of process.

Goal 3   I will be able to write expository paragraphs organized in the way of process.

Section 1   Writing a Good Paragraph (2) · · · · · · · · · ·

TASK ONE

Understanding Ways of Organization

ACTIVITY 1 ▶

Identifying paragraphs of process

Step 1

Work in pairs. Read the following paragraphs, and answer questions after your reading.

1. You can cook a perfectly boiled egg for breakfast if you follow these six easy steps. First, get a pot big enough to hold one egg. Then fill the pot 4/5 full with water and put in the egg. Next, turn the heat to high until the pot of water is boiling. Boil the egg in the water for three minutes. Take the egg out of the pot and put it in an egg cup. Now the egg is ready to eat. Enjoy it!

2. In old China a young man got married not of his own free will but through arrangements of his parents. First, his parents had to save enough money for the betrothal gifts and the wedding. Then they paid a matchmaker to look for a suitable woman or if they already had someone in mind, the matchmaker would go to the woman's family and talk with her parents about it. When both families were satisfied with the marriage, they would settle the engagement and choose the wedding day. After that, the man's family would set about painting and decorating the wedding chamber and sending invitations to relatives and friends. Finally a respectable person of the neighborhood was invited to marry the couple, who often had never seen each other until the wedding day.

3. Hurricanes are high-speed wind storms that start over the ocean and can have winds as fast as 250 kilometers per hour. Hurricanes usually happen over oceans, near the equator. They are formed when warm, wet air is forced upward by heavier, cold air. The air pressure drops quickly from the outer edge towards the center. This causes the wind speed to rise. The winds move in a circular pattern around the center, or "eye", of the hurricane. In the "eye", the winds stop and the clouds lift, but the ocean below remains violent. The average hurricane covers an area of at 240 kilometers. When the storm is over land, these winds destroy life and property.

Questions:
1. What is the purpose of writing each paragraph?
2. Is there a topic sentence(TS) in each paragraph? What are the topic and the main idea?
3. What similarities and differences can be found in the topics of the paragraphs?
4. What are the similarities in the specific details in the three paragraphs?
5. In what order are the supporting details organized in each paragraph?
6. How is each paragraph concluded?

Ways to organize expository paragraphs（3）

When you tell people how to do something or how something works or worked in chronological order or in logical steps, you are explaining a process.

• **Process**

A process paragraph explains how to perform a certain task or how something happens.

— **Directional process** gives a set of instructions or a step by step guidance on how to do something, usually in time order.

— **Informational process** provides information about how something works or how a particular event occurred, in time order or in logical order.

ACTIVITY 2 ▶

Identifying the specific ways of organization adopted

Step 1

Work in groups of 3 or 4. Read the information box above and identify the topic, the main idea and the specific type of process adopted in the following paragraphs.

4. To be a good friend, an individual has to spend time working on her friendships, or they will eventually fade. When two people first meet, they both need to be sure they are acting in good manner, so they don't scare the other away. After they meet and start talking a few times, they will start getting to know each other, calling each other, and spending more time with each other. That is how a friendship begins. After they call each other "friends", the friendship has to be made through the effort of more than just one person, so each has to do her own part. Friendships shouldn't take a lot of money but they do take a lot of time and care. Friends should always listen to what the other has to say, and then should give advice only when asked for it. No matter how much friends are alike, everyone has differences, so a friend should be able to accept their differences. After being a friend to a person for a long period of time, one might get tired of hearing repeated problems every day, but a good friend will always be there for her friend no matter what.

—by Denise Pafferty

Topic: _____

Main idea: _____

Type of process: _____

5. Uganda's economic fortunes have varied considerably over the past 40 years according to its political situation. After independence in 1962 and throughout the 1960s, Uganda showed great potential as one of the strongest economies in Sub-Saharan Africa. However, its performance was set back considerably during the subsequent periods of military rule (1971—1979) and civil war (1980—1985). Then, in 1987 the new National Resistance Movement (NRM) government under the leadership of President Yoweri Kaguta Museveni launched a recovery program to restore financial stability, create conditions for rapid and sustained growth and develop human capital. It also embarked on policy and institutional reform to deregulate the economy, eliminate direct state involvement in all but essential public services, and improve institutional efficiency. These efforts put Uganda on a path of recovery, but progress was slow through the early 1990s.

Topic: _____

Main idea: _____

Type of process: _____

6. People with flu can spread it to others up to about 6 feet away. Most experts think that flu viruses are spread mainly by droplets made when people with flu cough, sneeze or talk. These droplets can land in the mouths or noses of people who are nearby or possibly be inhaled into the lungs. Less often, a person might also get flu by touching a surface or object that has flu virus on it and then touching their own mouth or nose. Symptoms start 1 to 4 days after the virus enters the body. That means that you may be able to pass on the flu to someone else before you know you are sick, as well as while you are sick. Some people can be infected with the flu virus but have no symptoms. During this time, those persons may still spread the virus to others.

Topic: _____

Main idea: _____

Type of process: _____

TASK TWO
Understanding the Language Features

ACTIVITY 1 ▶

Analyzing and identifying language features

Step 1

Work in groups of 3 or 4. Read the 6 paragraphs in TASK ONE and answer the following questions.

1. What kind of information about the topic is given in the topic sentence(TS) of each paragraph, before starting explaining the specific process?

2. What transition words or phrases are used in each paragraph to indicate the order of actions or the process of doing things? Underline them in each paragraph.

3. When giving instructions or explanations, are the series of actions in each paragraph explained in active voice or passive voice? For what purposes?

4. Why are imperative sentences used in paragraph 1 in giving instructions?

5. Why are modal verbs used in paragraphs 4 and 6? Discuss and find out meanings different modal verbs can convey in writing.

Useful expressions for paragraph writing

• **Process**

—Beginning a Process: first, initially, to begin with, to start with, at first, first of all...

—Continuing the Process: second/third step, until, after(ward), then, next later, before, when, while, as soon as, as, upon, during, meanwhile...

—Ending a Process: finally, at last, the final step, eventually, the last step...

ACTIVITY 2 ▶

Rearranging sentences into a paragraph

Step 1

Work individually. Read the following sentences and rearrange the order of the sentences to make a process paragraph.

Using an Automatic Bank Machine

A. Enter the amount of cash you want.

B. Push the button next to "withdraw cash".

C. Insert your ATM card into the machine.

D. Take your cash, card, and your receipt.

E. Count the money to make sure the amount is correct.

F. Punch in your personal identification number.

G. Push the button next to the account you want to use.

Your answer: _____

Step 2

Add proper transition words or expressions to make the paragraph in Step 1 logical and coherent. Take the following sentence as the topic sentence of this paragraph.

Using an ATM is simple once you have learned these few steps.

You can also write your own topic sentence if you like.

Step 3

Check your partner's work.

1. The topic sentence in his/her paragraph writing is (perfect/OK/good) because

_____

_____ .

2. His/Her using of transition words or expressions is （perfect/OK/good）
because _____

_____ .

TASK THREE
Writing a Process Paragraph

Step 1

Practice writing a process paragraph on one of the following topics. Use one way of process（directional or informational process）in organizing your paragraph.

- The way a movie is made
- How ice melt
- How Internet addiction develops
- How to find a book in a library
- How to break an unhealthy habit
- How to shop cheaply
- How to shop online

Follow the steps listed below when writing your process paragraph.

1. Narrow the topic. Think of your audience and the information they need.
2. Make a topic sentence that clearly states the result of the process.
3. Free write some ideas that might help with the explanation of the process.
4. Drop unnecessary information that is not needed in the explanation.
5. List all necessary steps to complete the process.
6. Put all the steps in chronological order or logical order.
7. Include enough specific details to give thorough and clear explanation.
8. Use transition expressions to indicate order or time sequence.
9. Write a concluding sentence to restate the topic and wrap up the paragraph.
10. Revise and proofread for grammar, spelling and punctuation.

ASSIGNMENTS

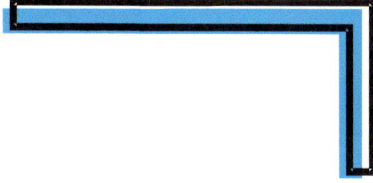

Write another process paragraph on another topic given in TASK THREE. Please use the other way of process (directional or informational process) in organizing your paragraph, which you didn't use in your writing practice in class.

Module 7 Writing an Expository Paragraph—Comparison and Contrast

When finishing the learning of this module,

Goal 1   I will understand the way of comparison and contrast in paragraph organization.

Goal 2   I will know language features in paragraphs of comparison and contrast.

Goal 3   I will be able to write expository paragraphs organized in the way of comparison and contrast.

Section 1   Writing a Good Paragraph (2)

TASK ONE

Understanding Ways of Organization

ACTIVITY 1 ▶

Identifying paragraphs of comparison and contrast

Step 1

Work in pairs. Read the following paragraphs, and answer questions after your reading.

1. Oceans and lakes have much in common, but they are also quite different. Both are bodies of water, but oceans are very large bodies of salt water, while lakes are much smaller bodies of fresh water. Lakes are usually surrounded by land, while oceans are what surround continents. Both have plants and animals living in them. The ocean is home to the largest animals on the planet,

whereas lakes support much smaller forms of life. When it is time for a vacation, both will make a great place to visit and enjoy.

2. Although there are a number of similarities, there are several differences between fast and home cooked meals. The first difference is that fast food is generally more fattening since oil is frequently used in the cooking process. In contrast, the fat content can be controlled in home cooking. Another important difference is the amount of time that each takes. Fast food is obviously quick since menus are limited and a number of staff are involved in the preparation and cooking process. However, home cooked meals take longer to complete since one person is usually responsible for the entire meal. The third difference is convenience. Fast food is ready-made and always available whereas home cooked meals are not instant.

3. My hometown and my college town have several things in common. First, my hometown Gridlock is a small town. It has a population of only about 10,000 people. Located in a rural area, Gridlock is surrounded by many acres of farmland which is devoted mainly to growing corn and soybeans. Gridlock also contains a college campus, Neutron College, which is famous for its Agricultural Economics program as well as for its annual Corn-Watching Festival. As for my college town, Subnormal, it too is small, having a population of about 11,000 local residents, which swells to 15,000 people when students from the nearby college are attending classes. Like Gridlock, Subnormal lies in the center of farmland which is used to raise hogs and cattle. Finally, Subnormal is similar to Gridlock in that it also boasts a beautiful college campus, called Quark College. This college is well known for its Agricultural Engineering department and also for its yearly Hog-calling contest.

Questions:
1. What is the purpose of writing each paragraph?
2. Is there a topic sentence(TS) in each paragraph? What are the topic and the main idea?
3. Which aspect does each paragraph mainly focus on, similarities or differences?
4. What supporting details are provided in each paragraph?
5. In what order are the supporting details organized in each paragraph? What general patterns can you conclude in the organization of similarities or differences?
6. How is each paragraph concluded?

> **Ways to organize expository paragraphs（4）**
>
> • **Comparison and contrast**
>
> A comparison and contrast paragraph either compares similarities or contrasts differences of things. Sometimes comparison and contrast appear together. There are two major ways of organizing paragraphs of comparison and contrast.
>
> — **Subject-by-subject comparison/contrast** examines one thing thoroughly, and then examines the other. The aspects examined in the two things should be identical and in the same order.
>
> — **Point-by-point comparison/contrast** examines two things at the same time, discussing them point by point.

ACTIVITY 2 ▶

Identifying specific ways of organization

Step 1

Work in groups of 3 or 4. Read the information box above and identify the topic, the main idea and the specific way of comparison and contrast（subject-by-subject or point-by-point）adopted in each of the following paragraphs.

4. Singers and Sisters

Jessica Simpson and Ashley Simpson are the same in a sense that they are both famous singers and even sisters, yet they are quite different in many ways. Jessica was always sure what she wanted to do with her life and worked very hard whereas Ashley enjoyed what life had to offer her at the moment. Jessica was in voice lessons and started to sing Gospel music during her high school career. On the other hand, Ashley took dance classes and learned how to perform to Hip-hop music. Jessica is more well known as the air head sister. For example, they both did a breath mint commercial together, and it poked fun of Jessica's blond moments by having Ashley point them out. Jessica is more "girly" of the sisters. She loves to wear dresses, high-heels, and has the blond bombshell look, unlike Ashley who has more of a punk style. Jessica Simpson's music has more of a classical pop tone, while Ashley's music has more of a pop-rock ring to it. Both of these girls are hard workers and both are very successful singers although they are very extraordinary in their own ways.

Topic: _____

Main idea: _____

Specific way of organization: _____

5. Even though Arizona and Rhode Island are both states of the U. S. , they are strikingly different in many ways. To begin with, the physical size of each state is different. Arizona is large, having an area of 114,000 square miles, whereas Rhode Island is only about a tenth the size, having an area of only 1,214 square miles. Another difference is in the size of the population of each state. Arizona has about four million people living in it, but Rhode Island has less than one million. The two states also differ in the kinds of natural environments that each has. For example, Arizona is a very dry state, consisting of large desert areas that do not receive much rainfall every year. However, Rhode Island is located in a temperate zone and receives an average of 44 inches of rain per year. In addition, while Arizona is a landlocked state and thus has no seashore, Rhode Island lies on the Atlantic Ocean and does have a significant coastline.

Topic: _____

Main idea: _____

Specific way of organization: _____

6. **Life Now and Life Five Years Ago**
My life now and my life five years ago are similar but there are also some major differences. Five years ago, I was living in Havre and going to high school. I didn't have to work because my parents supported me. I went to school every day and spent time with my friends. I babysat my nieces every day after school because both of my parents were working at the time. I had the responsibility of feeding my nieces and making sure nothing happened to them while I was watching them. I didn't really have any major goals five years ago. I wasn't really thinking about my future quite yet. On the other

hand, now I live in Great Falls and I'm not in high school anymore. I have to work now in order to support myself. I only work twenty hours a week because I'm in school right now. I have a lot more responsibilities now than I did five years ago. I have to take responsibilities for myself now and everything that I do. I have a lot of major goals now. For instance, I want to graduate and get my two-year degree. I want to come back and get a bachelor's degree. I have a lot of things that I want to accomplish now. Five years ago, I really wasn't going anywhere with my life, but now I'm starting to get my life in order and deciding what I want to do. In addition, I am still living at home with my parents and I still go to school. I still babysit my nieces every once in a while. I find time to spend with my family and friends. I still have some of the same responsibilities. I help my mom take care of my oldest niece. She has always lived with us, so I've always helped take care of her ever since she was a baby. Even though she is not a baby anymore, I still have to babysit her when my parents are gone because she is not quite old enough to stay by herself yet. I still have to depend on my parents for transportation because I don't have a vehicle right now. My life now has changed a lot in only five years.

Topic: _____

Main idea: _____

Specific way of organization: _____

TASK TWO
Understanding the Language Features

ACTIVITY 1 ▶

Analyzing and identifying language features

Step 1

Work in groups of 3 or 4. Read the 6 paragraphs in TASK ONE again, and answer the following questions.

1. How does each paragraph express the topic and the main idea in the topic sentence(TS)?

2. What transition words or expressions are used to indicate or to list similarities or differences? Underline these words and expressions in each paragraph.

3. Apart from indicating similarities or differences, what other roles do these transition words and expressions play in the writing of each paragraph?

4. How many major developing sentences are there in Paragraph 5? What's the relation between these major developing sentences and minor developing sentences?

5. Besides detailed explanations of similarities or differences, what other kinds of supporting details are given in these paragraphs?

Useful expressions for paragraph writing

- **Comparison and contrast**

1. Transition words and expressions used in making comparison:
   both, also, too, as well (as), like, just as ... so, similarly, is similar, the same, in the same way, as ... as ...

2. Transition words and expressions used in making contrast:
   however, although, but, yet, unlike, differ from, be different from, while, whereas, conversely, in contrast, on the other hand, on the contrary, not as ... as ... , not the same as ...

ACTIVITY 2 ▶

Using transition words or expressions properly

Step 1

Work individually. Read the following paragraph and choose proper transition words or expressions given below to fill in the blanks.

in the same way	likewise	similarly	too
both	another similarity	whereas	however
while	also		

Even though we come from different cultures, my wife and I are alike in several ways. For one thing, we are (1) _____ thirty-two years old. In fact, our birthdays are in the same month, hers on July 10 and mine on July 20. (2) _____ is that we both grew up in large cities. Helene was born and raised in Paris and I come from Yokohama. Third, our hobbies are alike (3) _____. My wife devotes a lot of her free time to playing jazz piano. (4) _____, I like to spend time after work strumming my guitar. A more important similarity concerns our values. For example, Helene has strong opinions about educating our children and raising them to know right from wrong. I feel (5) _____. Our children should receive a good education and also have strong moral training.

Step 2

Work in pairs. Read the following paragraph carefully, and then rewrite this paragraph of contrast by organizing the differences in the subject-by-subject way. Use proper transition words or expressions to make the paragraph logical and coherent.

Kevin and Amos differ in the way they approach life. One way the two men differ is that Kevin is an optimist while Amos is pessimistic about life. Kevin approaches each day anticipating the surprises and good things like his child understanding a difficult problem on her first attempt; however, Amos suspects something will go wrong like his car breaking down. In addition, Amos is conservative in his thinking for he believes government support makes people lazy; in contrast, Kevin holds liberal views believing that government can help people help themselves. Furthermore, Kevin likes to be in action and is always looking for something to do such as fixing things around his house or volunteering at school or in the community.

Step 3

Work with another pair and check each other pair's writing.

1. The topic sentence in their paragraph writing is (perfect/OK/not good) because _____

    _____.

2. The way of organization they use is (perfect/needs improving/not correct) because _____

    _____

3. Their using of transitions in making comparison and/or contrast is (perfect/ OK/not good) because _____

    _____.

TASK THREE
Writing a Comparison and Contrast Paragraph

Step 1

Practice writing a comparison and contrast paragraph on one of the following topics. Please use one way of comparison and contrast（subject-by-subject or point-by-point）in organizing your paragraph.

- Two roommates
- Two movies
- Two places you have visited
- Two fast-food restaurants
- A real vacation and a dream vacation
- Two close friends
- An active student and a passive student
- Two computer games

Follow the steps listed below when writing your paragraph.

1. Choose a topic and brainstorm on the similarities and/or differences.
2. Make a topic sentence that introduces the two subjects and the focus of your paragraph (similarities and/or differences).
3. Make a list of the similarities and/or differences, with supporting details.
4. Choose the specific way of organizing your comparison and contrast.
5. Write major developing sentences and minor developing sentences to explain similarities and/or differences.
6. Arrange the similarities and/or differences in an appropriate order.
7. Connect the developing sentences with transition words or expressions.
8. Write a concluding sentence to wrap up the paragraph.
9. Revise and proofread for grammar, spelling and punctuation.

ASSIGNMENTS

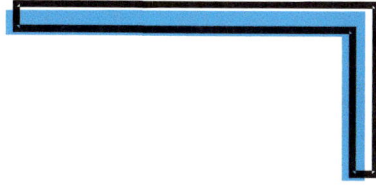

Practice writing another comparison and contrast paragraph on another topic given in TASK THREE. Please use the other way of comparison and contrast (subject-by-subject or point-by-point) in organizing your paragraph, which you didn't use in your writing practice in class.

Module 8 Writing an Expository Paragraph—Cause AND Effect

When finishing the learning of this module,

Goal 1   I will understand the way of Cause AND Effect in paragraph organization.

Goal 2   I will know language features in expository paragraphs of Cause AND Effect.

Goal 3   I will be able to write paragraphs organized in the way of Cause AND Effect.

Section 1   Writing a Good Paragraph (2)

TASK ONE

Understanding Ways of Organization

ACTIVITY 1 ▶

Identifying paragraphs of Cause AND Effect

Step 1

Work in pairs. Read the following paragraphs, and answer questions after your reading. While reading, think why the word "AND" in the title of this unit is capitalized.

1. **The Hard Life of Farmers**

The lack of rain and snow has horrible effects on farmers. With no rain their land dries up, and it is very difficult to grow anything. When the crops fail, the farmers haven't any choice but to get a second job in order to make the money they need. Farming is a full time job and with a second job, farmers are overworked, stressed and even depressed. Many farmers end up selling their land. Some farmers have accepted the government program the Conservation Reserve Program (CRP), which the land is left idle to let the grass grow and must be left idle a certain number of years. While the land is in the CRP program, some farmers have taken outside jobs. That is why when it doesn't rain, you notice that most of the farmers are very crabby. As a farmer's daughter, I have experienced some good times and some bad times. I have gained a great respect for farmers everywhere.

2. The depression was precipitated by the stock market crash in October 1929, but the actual cause of the crash was the collapse of an unhealthy economy. While the ability of the manufacturing industry to produce consumer goods had increased rapidly, mass purchasing power had remained relatively static. Most laborers, farmers, and white-collar workers, therefore, could not afford to buy the automobiles and refrigerators turned out by factories in the 1920s, because their incomes were too low. At the same time, the federal government increased the problem through economic policies that tended to encourage the very-rich to over-save.

3. **Why We Walk in Circles**?

It is a well-known fact that a person will move in a circle when he cannot use his eyes to control his direction. Pitch-dark nights, dense fogs, blinding snow-atoms, thick forests — all these can keep a traveler from seeing where he is going. Then he is unable to move in any fixed direction but walks in circles. Animals act the same way. You have probably heard the saying, "running around like a chicken with its head cut off." Blind birds fly in circles and a blind-folded dog swim in circles. Have you wound up a toy automobile and started it off across the floor? Then you know that it will rarely travel in a straight line. It will travel, instead, in some kind of arc, or curve. If it is to travel in a straight path, the wheel on both sides have to be exactly of equal size. If they are not, the little automobile turns toward the side with smaller wheels. Circular movement in walking is caused in much the same way. For most people, muscle development is not the same in both legs, so that the steps will be uneven. The difference may be so small that no one is aware of it. But small as it is, it can cause circular movement. By the same rule, a bird's wings do not develop evenly, and so it will fly in circles when blinded.

4. There are many reasons accounting for the fact that using disposable plastic bags would bring serious damage. Though it is so easy and convenient for people after shopping, using disposable plastic bags widely results in many environment problems. First of all, not only is using disposable plastic bags bad to our surrounding environment, but also it is harmful to our health. In addition, people will spend so much time and labor to deal with the issue. What's more, using disposable plastic bags wasted abundant resources. Shouldn't we take some measure to limit the use of disposable plastic bags? Therefore, it is high time that more attention be paid to how to solve the problem.

Questions:

1. What is the purpose of writing each paragraph?

2. Is there a topic sentence(TS) in each paragraph? What are the topic and the main idea?

3. What kind of logical relation does each paragraph want to explain? What is the difference between the logical relations explained in paragraphs 1 to 3 and in paragraph 4?

4. What supporting details are provided in each paragraph? What is the relation of the supporting details in paragraphs 1 to 3 and in paragraph 4?

5. In what order are the supporting details organized in each paragraph?

6. Which way of organization is adopted in paragraph 4? Explain your answer.

7. How is each paragraph concluded?

Ways to organize expository paragraphs (5)

Cause AND Effect

A Cause AND Effect paragraph interprets a causal chain or a series of cause and effect relation, by exploring the reasons for events and/or analyzing the consequences of occurrences.

The logical relation in this type of paragraphs can be shown in these ways:

- If CAUSE ... , then EFFECT ... ; EFFECT, if CAUSE.
- CAUSE, and thus EFFECT.

Recognizing the differences:

Cause AND effect paragraph interprets **a causal chain** or a domino effect, with an ordered sequence of events, in which any one event in the chain causes the next, as is shown in the diagram. There is immediate cause and ultimate cause in the chain.

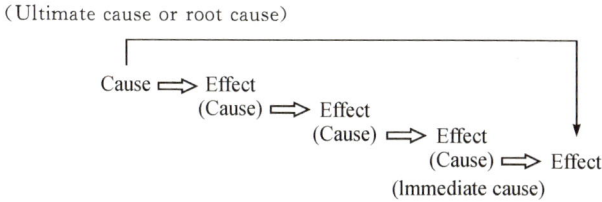

(Ultimate cause or root cause)

Cause ⟹ Effect
　　　(Cause) ⟹ Effect
　　　　　(Cause) ⟹ Effect
　　　　　　　(Cause) ⟹ Effect
　　　　　　　(Immediate cause)

Interpretation (cause OR effect) paragraph explains a causal relation and focus on either the cause(s) or the effect(s), sometimes with multiple causes leading to one effect or one cause leading to several effects, as is shown below.

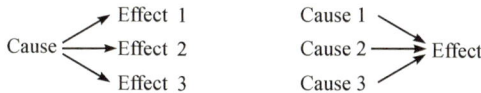

Cause → Effect 1
Cause → Effect 2
Cause → Effect 3

Cause 1 → Effect
Cause 2 → Effect
Cause 3 → Effect

ACTIVITY 2 ▶

Analyzing the causal relation

Step 1

Work in groups of 3 or 4. Read the two information boxes above and identify the way of organization (cause AND effect/interpretation-cause OR effect) adopted and the causal relation(s) in each paragraph in Activity 1.

Paragraph 1 Way of organization _____

Paragraph 2 Way of organization _____

Paragraph 3 Way of organization _____

Paragraph 4 Way of organization _____

TASK TWO
Understanding the Language Features

ACTIVITY 1 ▶

Analyzing and identifying language features

Step 1

Work in groups of 3 or 4. Read the 4 paragraphs in TASK ONE again, and answer the following questions.

1. How does each paragraph introduce the topic and the main idea in the topic sentence(TS)?

2. What transition words or expressions are used to indicate or to list the reasons or the effects? Underline these words and expressions in each paragraph.

3. Apart from indicating and connecting the causes and/or the effects, what other roles do these transition words or expressions play in the writing of each paragraph?

4. Identify the immediate and the ultimate causes of the effects in the causal chains in paragraphs 1 to 3. In which orders are these causes and effects organized?

5. Besides detailed explanations of the causes and/or the effects, what other kinds of supporting details are given in these paragraphs?

Useful expressions for paragraph writing

• **Cause AND Effect**

1. Transition words or expressions used to indicate **causes**:
   because, since, for, due to, owing to the fact that ... , the first cause (second, third), the first reason (second, third), yet another factor, ... is caused by, results from, one reason is that ... , etc.

2. Transition words or expressions used to indicate **effects**:
   so, therefore, leads to, consequently, hence, thus, then, next, as a result, one important effect is ... , another result, a third outcome, etc.

ACTIVITY 2 ▶

Using transition words or expressions properly

Step 1

Work in pairs. Read the following sentences and rearrange the order of the sentences to make a paragraph of Cause AND Effect.

A.　Moocs have become popular.

B.　More and more students are fond of online learning.

C.　Online learning has become a trend.

D.　Online learning makes learning free from the limitation of time and space.

E.　Students can learn the knowledge at any time and space

Your answer: _____

Step 2

Put the above sentences together to make a paragraph. Write a topic sentence and add proper transition words or expressions to make the paragraph logical and coherent.

_____

_____

_____

_____

_____

_____

_____

_____

_____

_____

TASK THREE
Writing a Cause AND Effect Paragraph

Step 1

Practice writing a Cause AND Effect paragraph on one of the following topics. Explain the causal chain relation in clear logic.

- Obesity in children/adults
- Parent involvement in schools
- Global warming
- Effects of divorce on children
- Cheating in exams

Follow the steps listed below when writing your Cause AND Effect paragraph.

1. Choose a topic and brainstorm on the causes or effects it has.
2. Write a topic sentence stating the topic and the focus (causes and/or effects).
3. Establish a series of cause and effect connection among the things listed, and be clear about the immediate and the ultimate causes.
4. Explain the cause and effect relations in a logical way.
5. Do not oversimplify, and include every significant cause or effect.
6. Provide enough supporting details and focus on the analyses of reasons or outcomes.
7. Use proper transition words or expressions to indicate the causes or the effects.
8. Explain the causal relation objectively, and avoid using first person pronouns or expressing personal opinion.
9. Write a concluding sentence of summary, suggestion, or prediction, etc.
10. Revise and proofread for grammar, spelling and punctuation.

ASSIGNMENTS

1. **Work in pairs. Read each other's paragraph writing in TASK THREE.**

   (1) Try to interpret the causal chain explained in your partner's paragraph.

   (2) Comment on each other's paragraph writing, and give suggestions for making improvements.

   (3) Improve your paragraph according to your partner's suggestions.

2. **Choose another topic and practice writing another Cause AND Effect paragraph. Follow the steps listed in TASK THREE when writing your paragraph.**

Module 9 Writing an Expository Paragraph—Problem-Solution

When finishing the learning of this module,

Goal 1   I will understand the way of problem-solution in paragraph organization.

Goal 2   I will know language features in expository paragraphs of problem-solution.

Goal 3   I will be able to write paragraphs organized in the way of problem-solution.

Section 1   Writing a Good Paragraph (2)

TASK ONE

Understanding Ways of Organization

ACTIVITY 1 ▶

Identifying paragraphs of problem-solution

Step 1

Work in pairs. Read the following paragraphs, and answer questions after your reading.

1. College graduates find it increasingly difficult to get a rewarding job. One reason perhaps is that many colleges and universities fail to adapt their courses to the development of economy. Second, there is an oversupply of graduates in certain specialties. What should be done to solve this problem? To begin with, colleges should get students out of the ivory tower and have their courses meet

the needs of industry and business so as to suit the on-going development of the national economy. Second, the government should provide college graduates with more opportunities to develop new skills. The third solution, I think, is to adopt strong measures of birth control because the greater the population, the less the opportunity for everyone to get a job. With these measures, some day in the near future college graduates will have less trouble when hunting for a job.

2. I keep a small notebook with me wherever I go. It has always been a frustrating experience for me to remember all the new words. To solve the problem, I made a small notebook to list all the important new words I come across in my reading. I review the new words whenever I have time, even on the way to our university library or the lunchroom. This helps a lot in remembering the new words.

3. As people live longer and the populations of developed countries grow older, several related problems can be anticipated. The main issue is that there will obviously be more people of retirement age who will be eligible to receive a pension. The proportion of younger, working adults will be smaller, and governments will therefore receive less money in taxes in relation to the size of the population. In other words, an aging population will mean a greater tax burden for working adults. Further pressures will include a rise in the demand for healthcare, and the fact that young adults will increasingly have to look after their elderly relatives. There are several actions that governments could take to solve the problems described above. Firstly, a simple solution would be to increase the retirement age for working adults, perhaps from 65 to 70. Nowadays, people of this age tend to be healthy enough to continue a productive working life. A second measure would be for governments to encourage immigration in order to increase the number of working adults who pay taxes. Finally, money from national budgets will need to be taken from other areas and spent on vital healthcare, accommodation and transport facilities for the rising numbers of older citizens. In conclusion, various measures can be taken to tackle the problems that are certain to arise as the populations of countries grow older.

4. We may carry about within ourselves the desire to make a good speech in public. But many of us lack self-confidence to make it as wished. To get over the barrier, we need to build up the courage to speak in front of others, such as answering questions in class and introducing ourselves to a group of

strangers. Then, we need to enrich ourselves with knowledge about what to be talked about as well as the art of delivering a speech in public. We need to put ourselves in the shoes of the public so as to know what we give will hold their interest. In brief, where there is a good preparation in advance, there is much chance of success in giving such a speech with confidence. In the end, more than we expect, we may discover in ourselves greater talents and confidence still unknown to us.

Questions:

1. What is the purpose of writing each paragraph?

2. Is there a topic sentence(TS) in each paragraph? What are the topic and the main idea?

3. What can be generalized about the ideas and details of these paragraphs?

4. How many parts can each paragraph be divided into? And what is each part mainly about, and in what order are the different parts organized in each paragraph?

5. How is each paragraph concluded?

Ways to organize expository paragraphs (6)

• **Problem-solution**

A problem-solution paragraph aims at suggesting proper ways to solve certain problems. It often starts by identifying a particular situation and then points out the problem(s). Afterwards, it proposes one or more solutions to cope with the problem(s). In some cases, there may be evaluation or comments on the solution(s) suggested, to bring the paragraph to an end.

ACTIVITY 2 ▶

Identifying specific information

Step 1

Work in groups of 3 or 4. Read the information box above and identify in each paragraph sentences which describe the situation, point out the problem(s), explain reasons for the problem(s) (if included), suggest solution(s), and make final comments or evaluations.

TASK TWO
Understanding the Language Features

ACTIVITY 1 ▶

Analyzing and identifying language features

Step 1

Work in groups of 3 or 4. Read the 4 paragraphs in TASK ONE again, and answer the following questions.

1. How does each paragraph explain the situation and point out the problem(s)?
2. How does each paragraph explain the purpose of writing and the main idea?
3. What transition words or expressions are used to help point out problem(s) and to suggest solution(s) to the problem(s)? Underline these words and expressions in each paragraph.

Useful expressions for paragraph writing

- **Problem-solution**
—to propose, to answer, to remedy, to solve, to cope with, to deal with, to fix, to handle
—solution, issue, problem, problematic, prevention, measure
—to solve the problem(s), to get over the barriers, to take measures/ actions . . .

ACTIVITY 2 ▶

Using transition words or expressions properly

Step 1

Work in pairs. Read the following sentences and rearrange the order of the sentences to make a paragraph of Problem-solution.

A. In response, the government has urged local villages to create more shared farmland.

B. Forests have been cut down at the rate of 278 square miles a year.

C. Observers say the program has succeeded in strengthening the country's agricultural base and bringing a new source of wealth to villagers.

D. The explosive growth of population in Ghana has led to removal of forests in much of the country.

E. It has sponsored the growing of cash crops and the planting of trees.

Your answer: _____

Step 2

Put the above sentences together to make a paragraph. Add proper transition words or expressions to make the paragraph logical and coherent.

_____

_____

_____

_____

_____

_____

_____

_____

TASK THREE
Writing a Problem-solution Paragraph

Practice writing a problem-solution paragraph on one of the following topics.

- Helping someone who is depressed
- Helping a friend make a good choice
- Getting out of a bad relationship
- Balancing studying and playing
- Preventing people from smoking in public places
- Fast food and its influence on healthy life
- Students' abilities to work and study simultaneously
- Improving students' health conditions

Follow the steps listed below when writing your problem-solution paragraph.

1. Choose a topic and brainstorm on the situation, problem, causes and solution.
2. Introduce the situation and describe the problem which needs to be dealt with.
3. Introduce the topic, the problem and/or solution(s) in a topic sentence.
4. Explain the solution(s) clearly, with specific details provided in proper order.
5. Give evidence to prove that the solution(s) is/are reasonable and effective.
6. Conclude by making evaluations or comments.
7. Revise and proofread for grammar, spelling and punctuation.

ASSIGNMENTS

1. **Work in pairs. Read each other's paragraph you write in class.**
   (1) Try to interpret the problem-solution relation in your partner's paragraph.
   (2) Comment on each other's paragraph writing, and give suggestions for making improvements.
   (3) Improve your paragraph according to your partner's suggestions.

2. **Choose another topic and practice writing another problem-solution paragraph. Follow the steps listed in TASK THREE when writing your paragraph.**

Module 10　Writing an Argumentative Paragraph

When finishing the learning of this module,

Goal 1　I will be able to identify an argumentative paragraph.

Goal 2　I will understand language features of argumentative paragraphs.

Goal 3　I will be able to write an argumentative paragraph.

Section 1　Writing a Good Paragraph (2)

TASK ONE
Understanding Ways of Organization

ACTIVITY 1 ▶

Identifying argumentative paragraphs

Step 1

Work in pairs. Read the following paragraphs, and answer questions after your reading.

Paragraph 1

　　Canada is one of the best countries in the world to live in. First, Canada has an excellent health care system. All Canadians have access to medical services at a reasonable price. Second, Canada has a high standard of education. Students are taught by well-trained teachers and are encouraged to continue studying at university. Finally, Canada's cities are clean and efficiently managed. Canadian cities have many parks and lots of space for people to live. As a result, Canada is a desirable place to live.

Paragraph 2

I think this states should require automobile drivers and passengers to wear seat belts. Safety tests prove that people are less likely to be hurt badly in an automobile accident if they are wearing seat belts. Thirty-two states have already passed laws requiring people to wear seat belts. Those seat belt laws have reduced traffic-related deaths. Some people may say that seat belts are uncomfortable or a bother. I think that is a small price to pay for added safety. It all comes down to one thing: Seat belts save lives!

Paragraph 3

I believe that I should be hired as a waiter in your restaurant. Because I worked as a waiter last summer in Ann's Dinner in Seattle, I have had the necessary experience. In fact, before I left Ann's Dinner to return to school, I was chosen "Outstanding Employee of the Month." Both the owner, Jill Johnson, and her customers stated that I was a friendly, speedy worker. I never missed a day of work, and I always arrived on the job early. I enjoy being a waiter and believe that I could do an excellent job in your restaurant.

Paragraph 4

The cost of having technology in schools is very high, and the cost will only increase in the future. Computers help students do their homework. However, they cost the United States a lot of money. Right now, technology in schools costs about $3 billion. This is $70 per student. The government is planning to put $15 billion into schools, or about $300 per student. It will cost about $11 billion to give every public school a lab with 25 computers to every 5 students. Technology in schools proves to have a very costly future.

Questions:

1. What is the purpose of writing each paragraph? What is the difference between the purposes of paragraphs 1 and 4 and paragraphs 2 and 3?

2. Is there a topic sentence (TS) in each paragraph? Underline the topic and the main idea.

3. Does the TS of each paragraph state a fact or express an opinion? Give your reasons.

4. Is the writer objective or subjective in writing each paragraph? Give your reasons.

5. What kinds of specific details are provided in each paragraph? Give examples.

6. How are the developing sentences organized in each paragraph? In what order? Explain your answer.

7. How is each paragraph concluded?

8. What else do the concluding sentences of paragraphs 2 and 3 express? For what purpose(s)?

Step 2

Work in groups of 3 or 4. Discuss and summarize features of argumentative paragraphs.

1. Purpose of writing: _____

2. Topic: _____

3. Controlling idea: _____

4. Supporting details: _____

5. Concluding sentence: _____

6. General tone of writing: _____

Argumentative paragraphs

An argumentative or persuasive paragraph argues for or against an idea or tries to persuade readers of a specific point of view. It should be built around one main idea or one **argument**, which should be stated clearly at the beginning. **Supporting points/Major supporting ideas** and **supporting details/ minor supporting details** (examples, facts, statistics, authorities, etc.) should be provided to convince the readers that the point of view stated is the best and correct one.

ACTIVITY 2 ▶

Identifying specific information

Step 1

Work in pairs. Read the information box above and find out the argument, the supporting points and supporting details in each of the four paragraphs in Activity 1.

Step 2

Work in groups of 3 or 4. Analyze the following paragraphs by identifying the topic, the argument, the supporting points and the type(s) of supporting details in each paragraph.

Paragraph 5

The poodle makes a perfect pet because poodles offer their owners a companionship for life, not to mention that they have a loveable personality. Poodles are sweet, smart, playful, and well-mannered and they love to be around people. They are always willing to lend their unquestionable love and loyalty when you need the most and they are yours for life. Apart from being a happy spirited dog and a great companion, the poodle is small and doesn't require a lot of room, so they are ideal for apartments or city settings. The poodle is suited to most environments and lifestyles; whether it be living in the suburbs or downtown, with one person or a couple, or even living with a family and children, the poodle fits right in. The poodle is a dog that warms your heart with its character. It becomes a part of your family no matter where you live and it can provide you with love and companionship that you won't want to do without. In fact, you can't ask for a better dog.

Topic: _____

Argument: _____

Supporting points:

1. _____

2. _____

3. _____

Types of supporting details: _____

Paragraph 6

Alexander the Great was a successful ruler because his actions created long lasting effects on cultures that continue to the present day. One example of his legacy was the creation of a Hellenistic society. Hellenism was the combination of Greek, Persian, and Egyptian cultures. During this remarkable time period, people were encouraged to pursue a formal education and produce many different kinds of art. New forms of math, science, and design made great impacts on society. If this new way of life had not been as successful as it was, Alexander's legacy would not be as memorable and groundbreaking. Because he conquered many countries and blended together many different cultures, Alexander the Great is widely recognized for his achievements and credited with being one of the greatest rulers in history.

Topic: _____

Argument: _____

Supporting points:

1. _____

2. _____

3. _____

Types of supporting details: _____

Paragraph 7

I do well in school, and people think I am smart because of it. But it's not true. In fact, three years ago I struggled in school. However, two years ago I decided to get serious about school and made a few changes. First, I decided I would become interested in whatever was being taught, regardless of what other people thought. I also decided I would work hard every day and never give up on any assignment. I decided to never, never fall behind. Finally, I decided to make school a priority over friends and fun. After implementing these changes, I became an active participant in classroom discussions. Then my test scores began to rise. I still remember the first time that someone made fun of me because "I was smart." How exciting! It seems to me that being smart is simply a matter of working hard and being interested. After all, learning a new video game is hard work even when you are interested. Unfortunately, learning a new video game doesn't help you get into college or get a good job.

Topic: _____

Argument: _____

Supporting points:

1. _____

2. _____

3. _____

Types of supporting details: _____

TASK TWO
Understanding the Language Features

ACTIVITY 1 ▶

Analyzing and identifying language features

Step 1

Work in groups of 3 or 4. Read the 7 paragraphs in TASK ONE again, and answer the following questions.

1. How does each paragraph state its argument?
2. Identify major developing sentences for supporting points and minor developing sentences for supporting details in paragraph 1. What are the differences in the

ideas or information the sentences convey and the roles they play in the paragraph?

3. What transition words or expressions are used to introduce different supporting points and supporting details? Underline these words and expressions in each paragraph.

4. What transition words or expressions are used to give examples? Underline these words and expressions in paragraphs with examples.

ACTIVITY 2 ▶

Using transition words or expressions properly

Step 1

Work in pairs. Read the following paragraph and choose proper transition words or phrases given below to fill in the blanks.

in my opinion	and	finally	consequently
in addition	for example	although	therefore
first of all	for instance		

Around the globe, children often use computers from a very young age. (1) _____ it is important for children to participate in various well-balanced activities, (2) _____ children who use the computer daily are actually developing a skill for future success. (3) _____, from a personal point of view, computers are an invaluable resource to help young people explore the world around them. (4) _____, children who use the Internet to satisfy their curiosity about diverse topics are already becoming independent learners. (5) _____ by starting early in their lives, children feel totally at ease around computers; they are also able to take advantage of the wide range of services computers provide. (6) _____, from an academic viewpoint, children have no choice but to master this technological invention. (7) _____, when I was in university, students brought their laptops to class to take notes, do research and exchange information. (8) _____, children who build confidence and experience in these abilities are at a distinct advantage over those who have not.

(9) _____, from a professional perspective, the computer has found a permanent place in the workplace. Today, employers still pay to provide computer training to their employees. Tomorrow, corporations will expect prospective job applicants to already possess these critical job skills. (10) _____, parents who encourage their children to use the computer for a reasonable period of time daily are in fact investing in the children's future career.

TASK THREE
Writing an Argumentative Paragraph

Step 1

Practice writing an argumentative paragraph on one of the following topics.

- Should restaurants be required to include calories on all menu items?
- Should an added tax be placed on sugary drinks, such as sodas?
- Are cameras in public places an invasion of privacy?
- Should teens be allowed to have cosmetic surgery?
- Is there too much pressure on teenagers to go to college?
- Can online dating replace meeting a person in real life?
- Can video games be a useful learning tool?
- Should parents pay children for good grades?
- Is it okay for parents to monitor teens' Internet use?

Step 2

Follow the steps listed below when writing an argumentative paragraph.

1. Choose a topic and decide on your argument in the paragraph.
2. Brainstorm ideas and evidence to support your argument.
3. Write a topic sentence with your argument clearly stated.
4. Select significant points and relevant details to support your opinion.

5. Write major developing sentences to indicate different supporting points to convince readers of the argument.

6. Add minor developing sentences to provide details to support different supporting points.

7. Use proper transition words or expressions to connect the sentences.

8. Conclude the paragraph by drawing a conclusion, restating your argument, giving suggestions, making a prediction or asking for immediate action, etc.

9. Revise and proofread for grammar, spelling and punctuation.

ASSIGNMENTS

1. **Work in pairs. Read each other's paragraph you write in class.**

   (1) Identify the argument, the supporting points and supporting details in your partner's paragraph.

   (2) Comment on each other's paragraph writing, and give suggestions for making improvements.

   (3) Improve your paragraph according to your partner's suggestions.

2. **Choose another topic given in TASK THREE and practice writing another argumentative paragraph. Follow the steps listed in TASK THREE when writing your paragraph.**

Module 11 Writing a Paragraph with Exemplification and Listing

When finishing the learning of this module,

Goal 1 I will understand the use of exemplification and listing in paragraph writing.

Goal 2 I will know language features in paragraphs with exemplification or listing used.

Goal 3 I will be able to write paragraphs with exemplification or listing used.

Section 1 Writing a Good Paragraph (2)

TASK ONE

Understanding Ways of Organization

ACTIVITY 1 ▶

Identifying types of paragraphs

Step 1

Work in pairs. Read the following paragraphs, and identify the purpose and the type (narrative, descriptive, expository or argumentative) of each paragraph. Find out the topic, the main idea and the kind(s) of supporting details (examples, facts, statistics, or specific information, etc.) in each paragraph.

Paragraph 1

John was only five years old, but he was extremely smart for his age. He wasn't that tall and he was a bit on the skinny side. He had big blue eyes, light brown hair, rosy cheeks, and a friendly smile. Just looking at him he seemed like any other kid—quite normal. Yet, everyone in his class looked at him differently because John could never be a normal kid. Instead, he wasn't normal. No, he was a genius.

Purpose of writing: _____

Type of paragraph: _____

Topic: _____

Main idea: _____

Type(s) of supporting details: _____

Paragraph 2

　　Taiwan's coastal geography greatly influences Taiwanese cuisine. Taiwan is an island, and fishing has traditionally supplied an abundance of fresh fish and seafood. Oysters are an especially common ingredient in Taiwanese food. They appear in dishes such as oyster omelet and oyster vermicelli, both of which are popular street foods. The ready availability of such shellfish makes them a staple in Taiwanese cuisine. Also popular are skewers of marinated, grilled squid, often sold by street vendors. Being on an island, Taiwan treats seafood not as an occasional delicacy but as an everyday snack.

Purpose of writing: _____

Type of paragraph: _____

Topic: _____

Main idea: _____

Type(s) of supporting details: _____

Paragraph 3

　　I favor Christmas time because of the cool, chilling weather. I love the feeling of the cool, crisp wind blowing through my hair. When it's cold outside, it just makes the inside of your house feel much cozy. One Christmas I especially remember because it snowed. My brother, my dad, my mom, and I spent all day building a snowman and having snowball fights. Our cheeks were rosy, our hands and feet were numb, and our noses were as red as Rudolph's. When we went inside, we all sat by the fire and drank hot chocolate and laughed about the fights we had in the snow. That was the best Christmas ever.

Purpose of writing: _____

Type of paragraph: _____

Topic: _____

Main idea: _____

Type(s) of supporting details: _____

Paragraph 4

Yesterday, we really had a hard time getting Peter out of the well he had fallen into. First, we fashioned a rope by linking our belts together. Then, we lowered it to Peter, telling him to grasp the end. After he had hold of the belt-rope, we began to pull him slowly, inch by inch, out of the well. During his ascent, no one dared speak a word. Finally, we could grasp his arms, and with a shout of relief, we pulled him out onto the grassy bank.

Purpose of writing: _____

Type of paragraph: _____

Topic: _____

Main idea: _____

Type(s) of supporting details: _____

ACTIVITY 2 ▶

Understanding paragraph organizations with exemplification or listing used

Step 1

Work in groups of 3 or 4. Read the following expository paragraphs, and find out the specific way of organization adopted and the kind(s) of supporting details in each paragraph.

Paragraph 5

There are some distinct similarities between fast food and home cooked meals. The first similarity is that they both provide a variety of choices. There are a number of selections available in restaurants; salads, burgers, sandwiches and more. Similarly, if the ingredients are available, anything can be cooked in your own kitchen. Another similarity is that each can be relatively inexpensive. Fast food can be very cheap since many meals are under five dollars. In the same way, home cooked meals also can be reasonable especially if ingredients are carefully considered for the cost. Thirdly, both fast food and home cooked meals can be delicious. We know that many people enjoy the taste of fast food because it is popular around the world. Likewise, home cooked meals can certainly be yummy if they are prepared just as you like them.

Topic: _____

Main idea: _____

The specific way of organization: _____

Type(s) of supporting details: _____

Paragraph 6

Some freshmen feel that they are not as passionate or energetic as before. They are getting tired more easily than before. They are showing signs of a lack of energy and depression. A lack of restful sleep because of tests, peer pressure and problems with relationships can also spell trouble. To solve this problem, all sides concerned should take joint measures. First, schools and teachers may give students immediate guidance. In addition, parents and friends could offer adequate help. Finally, students themselves need to arrange time better and avoid stress. As a result, these efforts will make freshmen passionate and energetic again.

Topic: _____

Main idea: _____

The specific way of organization: _____

Type(s) of supporting details: _____

Paragraph 7

  There are problems in applying this approach. First, ability to pay is sometimes difficult to measure. Poverty can be transitory. For example, those in need of social care services may be in transitory poverty. Forcing them to pay could reduce their ability to get out of poverty. Second, some problems are catastrophic in nature. In such cases, the expenditure is great, so that having to pay out of pocket for services would push the non-poor into poverty. Examples of catastrophic problems include a disabling accident, the onset of disease, or illness affecting more than one family member at the same time.

Topic: _____

Main idea: _____

The specific way of organization: _____

Type(s) of supporting details: _____

Paragraph 8

  Now TV has become necessary in our life. We can get all kinds of information through TV such as the weather, information, or laws, knowledge and so on. We can watch some funny programs to relax and make us happy. The distance between countries is shortened with the help of TV. We can get to know all kinds of events around the world. Though TV is good for us, sometimes it has bad influence. Some students spend so much free time in watching TV that they have no time to study. It influences their lessons. And some programs are not good for children. As far as I'm concerned, we should choose proper programs at proper time for people in different ages, especially for children.

Topic: _____

Main idea: _____

The specific way of organization: _____

Type(s) of supporting details: _____

TASK TWO

Understanding Exemplification and Listing
in Writing

Step 1

Work in groups. Go over the 8 paragraphs in TASK ONE and answer the following questions.

1. What types of supporting details are generally provided in these different types of paragraphs?
2. Why are these types of details provided in writing? For what purposes?
3. How are these details added in each paragraph? What kinds of transition words or expressions are used? Underline these words and expressions in each paragraph.
4. What are the differences between the use of exemplification or listing and the use of different ways of organization we learned in previous modules?

Ways of providing details in paragraph writing

1. **Exemplification:** providing details by giving examples
2. **Listing:** explaining a list of things one by one

Useful expressions for paragraph writing

1. **Exemplification:** for example, such as, for instance, like, one example is ... , ... is a good example, take ... as an example
2. **Listing:** first (ly), second (ly), third (ly), another, finally, lastly, besides, in addition, what's more ...

Step 2

Work in pairs. Complete each of the following paragraphs by choosing the best transition words or expressions to fit in each blank.

1. A vegetarian can be defined as someone who does not eat meat, fish, or other animal products, such as eggs or cheese; _____ , he or she eats vegetables,

fruits, grains, and seeds. _____ this diet consists of non-meat food sources, a vegetarian typically consumes less fat and cholesterol than an individual who consumes meat. _____, raising animals for food uses valuable land, water, and energy. _____, adopting a vegetarian diet helps conserve the valuable resources that our future depends on.

A. consequently   B. because   C. furthermore

D. instead   E. for example

2. _____ many educators and parents have praised the Harry Potter series, some Christian parents have called for a ban on the books in their schools and libraries. Some churches have even gone as far as burning the books, citing biblical injunctions against witchcraft, _____ those in Exodus and Leviticus. _____, some Christians believe the books are compatible with Christianity, _____, that they embody basic Christian beliefs.

A. although   B. in addition   C. such as

D. however   E. indeed

3. Massive energy consumption is having a negative impact on the planet. _____, in the summer of 2006, Western Europe experienced some of the hottest weather on record. _____, this temperature increase is not an isolated occurrence. _____, almost every credible scientist today believes that the earth is experiencing climate change due to the emissions of greenhouse gases from cars and coal-burning power plants. Ninety percent of the energy used in the U. S. comes from fossil fuels, oil, coal, and natural gas (Borowitz 43), _____ problems arise from other sources, too (e. g., nuclear power plants leave radioactive by-products, making storage difficult). _____, dams are not much better, as nearby populations must be relocated, and the surrounding habitat is destroyed.

A. in fact   B. for example   C. unfortunately

D. moreover   E. but

4. _____, studies investigating the pros and cons of single-sex versus coeducation schools have come to public attention, _____ the results show some dramatic differences between the genders. _____, single-sex schools appear to help girls with their work habits; _____, boys achieve a higher success rate in a coeducational system. _____, girls seem to work best when communication and co-operation are stressed, _____ boys may be more comfortable with individual and competitive styles of learning.

A. whereas   B. for example   C. by contrast

D. recently   E. and   F. in other words

Step 3

Work in pairs. Fill in blanks in the following paragraph with sentences or expressions to provide supporting details. Make use of exemplification or listing with proper transition words or expressions used.

For a university student in China, living on the campus is beneficial to his study. Firstly, the atmosphere can help to make him feel pressed and therefore work hard. _____

_____

He may even find students practicing English on the way to the classroom.

_____

_____.

The student does not have to worry about any traffic jam or the long hour from home to school. And with all his classmates living in the same quarter, he can easily find someone with whom he can discuss the problems he comes across in study whenever he has one. _____

_____.

Thirdly, living at school may provide the student many chances for academic activities, _____

_____

which benefits his professional career. For all these advantages, many students choose to stay on the campus rather than living at home.

TASK THREE
Writing Paragraphs Using Exemplification
or Listing

Step 1

Develop the following topic sentences into unified, coherent and complete paragraphs by organizing the paragraphs in the ways stated in the brackets.

1. Having a hobby is something which can bring you great benefits.

    (Interpretation-cause or effect / exemplification)

2. Swimming and running have both similarities and differences.

    (Comparison and contrast / Listing)

3. I can't stand up with the hot summer in my hometown.

    (Description / Listing)

4. Family is very important to everyone. To me, family is...

    (Extended definition / Listing / Exemplification)

ASSIGNMENTS

Choose 2 topics and practice writing paragraphs by organizing them in different ways. Combine the use of exemplification or listing in your writing.

- Our classroom / Our school / My bedroom
- How to lose weight without losing mind?
- Strawberries vs. Apples
- My favorite gift
- A right choice
- What makes my parents special?
- True friendship
- Leaving home for the first time
- High school graduates should take a year off before entering college.
- People have become overly dependent on technology.
- Participating in team sports helps to develop good character.
- Students should/shouldn't be required to take physical education courses.

SECTION 2

Writing Letters for Practical Purposes

Module 12　Basic Elements and Formats of English Letters

When finishing the learning of this module,

Goal 1　I will know basic elements of English letters.

Goal 2　I will know different types of English letters.

Goal 3　I will be able to format different types of English letters.

Section 2　Writing Letters for Practical Purposes · · · · · · · · · ·

TASK ONE

Identifying Basic Elements of English Letters

Step 1

Discuss the following questions in pairs.

1. When do people write letters, and for what purposes?
2. What different types of letters do you know?
3. What do you know about the elements and formats of different types of English letters?

Step 2

Read the following letters individually and find out the basic elements and format in each letter.

Letter 1

July 1, 2014

Dear Katie,

I hope you are settled in comfortably in Manchester. I miss you already! But I know your new position will open up a lot of career opportunities for you. It's also great that you'll be closer to your family. And, at least for now, it's still warm!

I too have some good job news. My former boss just told me about a great position at her new company. I would still be doing administrative duties but would be managing the whole office, and it'd include a nice pay rise too. She says she's already spoken highly of me to the person I'd be working for, so I think there's a good chance it will come through.

Besides that, everything else is going pretty well.

I'm already looking forward to seeing you in December. As soon as the tickets for the winter extravaganza go on sale, I'll book us a couple of tickets. Let me know if Rob decides to come, too — if so, I'll make it three. Let's talk soon!

Until next time,

Jane

Letter 2

Ms. Susan Harris

Lockwood Middle School

307 Main Street

Lockwood, NJ 51686

December 10, 2008

Mrs. Jody Coling,

President

Lockwood Health Association

23 Main Street

Lockwood, NJ 51678

Dear Mrs. Coling,

My name is Susan Harris and I am writing on behalf of the students at Lockwood Middle School.

A significant amount of the students at the school have been working on a project which relates to the unemployment problem within the youth demographic of Lockwood. You are invited to attend a presentation that will be held within the media room of the school where a variety of proposals that will demonstrate the ability of the community to develop employment opportunities for the youth within the community.

At the presentation, there will be several students receiving awards which will recognize them within the community from the Mayor. Refreshments will also be available at the presentation.

As one of the prominent figures in the community, we would be honored by your attendance. Our special presentation will be held at our school auditorium on January 16th. Please reply by Monday the 9th of January to confirm your attendance to the function.

We look forward to seeing you there.

Sincerely,

Ms. Susan Harris

Ms. Susan Harris

Enclosure (1) : Brochure

Letter 3

The Graduate School
Hawaii University
P. O. Box 553
Hawaii, U. S. A
July 25, 1999

Foreign Affairs Office
Southwest Jiaotong University
Chengdu, Sichuan Province
P. R. China

Dear Sirs:

I am a graduate student at the Graduate School of Hawaii University concentrating my studies on the People's Republic of China. Upon graduation, I would like to come to your country as an English instructor or tutor at your university.

I have been studying the Chinese language and culture for the past ten months and will continue to do so until my graduation in August of 2000. I would then like to continue my studies in China as an English instructor. In addition to my extensive educational background, I have computer and basketball coaching experiences which, I guess, may also be of benefit to you.

Enclosed is a resume highlighting my educational background.

I look forward to your earliest possible reply. Please feel free to respond in Chinese characters.

With Best Regards
Sincerely yours,
John W. White
John W. White

Letter 4

June 9, 2010

Dear Sir or Madam,

I'm writing to complain about the refrigerator which arrived on June 1. We find there is something wrong with the refrigeration facilities. After we used it for several days, we found that food stored in the refrigerating compartment went bad quickly. When we finally decided to take the temperature of it, we were surprised to find it was around 15 ℃, far from the standard temperature ranging from 0 ℃ to 9 ℃.

This problem has affected our normal life. Would you please let me know whether or not you can send a repairman as soon as possible? I hope that my problem will get your kind consideration.

Yours faithfully,
Rose Wang

Step 3

Work in groups of 3 to 4 and discuss the following questions.

1. What types of letter do these letters belong to, formal letters or friendly letters?

2. What are the differences between the two types of letters?

3. What basic elements have you found in these letters, including the optional ones? What kinds of information should be provided for each element?

- _____

- _____

- _____

- _____

- _____

- _____
- _____
- _____

4. What differences have you found in the basic elements of the two types of letters?

Basic elements of English letters:

- **Heading:** Including the return address (optional) and the date
- **Inside address:** Including the recipient's address (usually omitted in friendly letters)
- **Salutation:** Including the name (and the title in formal letters) of the recipient
- **Body:** The main text, including information or feeling the writer wants to convey
- **Closing:** E. g. _Your friend_, _Sincerely_, _Yours_, _Kind regards_, _Yours truly_, ...
- **Signature:** The writer's name
- **Enclosure** (when necessary): Including information about the things enclosed

---

Types of letters for different purposes:

- Application letters
- Apology letters
- Appeal letters
- Complaint letters
- Congratulation letters
- Confirmation letters
- Cover letters
- Invitation letters
- ...

- Love letters
- Marketing letters
- Recommendation letters
- Request letters
- Reference letters
- Sales letters
- Enquiry letters
- Thank-you letters
- ...

TASK TWO
Understanding Formats of English Letters

ACTIVITY 1 ▶

Finding out formats of different types of letters

Step 1

Discuss in groups of 3 to 4 and answer the following questions.

1. What are the differences in the formats of the four letters given in TASK ONE?
2. Where and how are the address, the date, and the salutation written in each letter? What differences can you find in these letters?
3. How are punctuations (comma and colon) and capitalization used in these letters?
4. How are indentation, alignment and blank lines used in these letters? What general types of format can be found in these letters?
5. How are contractions used in these letters? Why?

Step 2

Work in groups and summarize the formats of the two general types of letters by completing the table below.

Elements	Format in friendly letters	Format in formal letters
Return address	Optional	Sender's name, title (when necessary) _____ Name of the company _____ City, state, zip code _____ Street address on one line

Elements	Format in friendly letters	Format in formal letters
Date	Left-aligned or _____ _____ _____ _____ (*July* 1, 2019)	Left-aligned, single spaced, month-day-year format, with month in a word, day and year in numbers, comma after day
Inside address	Optional	Recipient's name, title _____ Name of company _____ City, state, zip code _____ Street address _____
Salutation	Left-aligned, first or full name (*Dear Kate*,)	Left-aligned, _____ (*Dear Sir*, /*Mr.* /*Mrs.* ...,)
Closing		
Name	First name or full name	Full name and title
Contractions		Shouldn't be used
Comma used	After salutation, _____	
Indentation	First line of a paragraph indented	
Alignment		Paragraphs Left-aligned, single spaced
Blank lines	Between date/salutation, paragraphs, _____ _____ _____	

Formats of letters:

- **Block format:** All elements left-aligned, and paragraphs separated with blank lines

- **Modified block format:** Date, sign off and signature beginning at the center point of the page line, beginning of paragraphs indented, and paragraphs single or double spaced

- **Semi-block format:** All elements left-aligned, with beginning of each paragraph indented, and paragraphs double spaced

- **Indented format:** Return address on top right side, recipient's address and date below left-aligned, beginning of paragraphs indented, paragraphs single or double spaced, closing, sign off and signature at the bottom right side of the letter

ACTIVITY 2 ▶

Formating different types of letters properly

Step 1

Put the information provided in the following boxes in proper places and formats in the letter forms below, and add commas where necessary.

Letter 1

Customer Service Department, Sullivan Office Furniture Company
1432 Bradley Boulevard, Muskegon, Michigan 49441
July 12, 2019
Dear Sir or Madam:
157 John Street, New York, New York 10038
Yours sincerely,
Jane Fulton
Office Manager

Letter 2

125 South Street

Brattleboro，Vermont 05301

Manager Service Dept.

David Drew

National Electronics Company

309 Fourth St.

Pipe Creek，Texas 78063

Dear Mr. Drew，

February 26，2019

Sincerely，John Wright

_____

_____

_____

_____

_____

_____

_____

_____

_____

_____

_____

Letter 3

sender：Li Ming
country：P. R. China
zip code：430079
city：Wuhan
house number：156
province：Hubei
road name：Luoyu Road
apartment number：302
date：2020/11/18

receiver：Mary Smith
state：California
house number：228
zip code：94002
store name：Olympic Shoe Store
road name：Athens Way
country：U. S. A.
city：Oakland

ASSIGNMENTS

Work in pairs and format the required elements in the following letters.

1. You are writing an invitation letter to the headmaster of your middle school.

Main Text

2. You are writing a thank-you letter to your friend.

Main Text

Module 13 Writing Different Types of Friendly/Personal Letters

When finishing the learning of this module,

Goal 1   I will know the roles of different parts in the body section of a friendly/personal letter.

Goal 2   I will know some useful expressions in writing different types of friendly/personal letters.

Goal 3   I will know how to write different types of friendly/personal letters properly.

Section 2   Writing Letters for Practical Purposes • • • • • • • • • •

TASK ONE

Understanding Roles of Different Parts
in a Letter

Step 1

Read the following letters and analyze the organization and language use in each letter.

1. **Congratulation Letter**

> Dear Joanna,
>
> How wonderful it is to hear that you'll be a mother soon. Congratulations! What are you hoping for, a boy or a girl? Or both?! Perhaps you'll inspire me to have a go, but I think I'll wait to have a peep at yours first before taking the plunge.
>
> Say hello to Martin and tell him to get prepared for fatherhood.
>
> Love,
> Susan

2. Apology letter

68 Pine Zaggat Lane

Hampervile，NE 25385

January 5，2005

Dear Jolene，

I am sorry about forgetting about our lunch date. It was completely my fault; I was so busy at work that it must have slipped my mind. How about I treat you to lunch next Wednesday at the new Italian restaurant Julie's at 12：30PM? I have marked this date in my planner so I will not forget about it. I'd just like to apologize again for missing the lunch date.

Your friend，

Cathy

3. Invitation letter

97 Fir Crescent

Denver，CO 80409

December 17，2008

Dear Mr. and Mrs. Johnson，

As the parents of the bride，I would like to take this opportunity to invite you to the wedding of our daughter，Sandra Green to her fiancé，Adam Locke. On this joyous occasion，we wish to share the day with our closest friends and family members.

Children grow faster than any of us can imagine，the time is upon us to watch our child grow and flourish into a new stage of their life. He proposed while the two of them were on vacation，she happily accepted and now they are to be married.

The formal event will be located at the Fire Lake Golf and Country Club on the fifteenth of August at three o'clock，two thousand and nine.

Please RSVP by the fifteenth of June to ensure attendance.

We hope to see you there to enjoy this special day with friends and family.

Sincerely yours,
John Smith

4. Letter of refusing an invitation

Dear Sue,

Thank you for your invitation to party on Friday. Unfortunately, I have already made other arrangements then and can't cancel them—Tony and Joanna have invited me over. It means I'll be away all weekend, but I'll give you a call when I get back and you can tell me how it went.

Hope you have fun.

Love,
Robert

5. Thank-you letter

Hi Aunt Kelly!

Thanks for the new bike you bought me for my birthday; it's just what I wanted. The color red fits the bike well! It is my favorite color. I plan on riding the bike around my neighborhood everyday right after school. I look forward to seeing you soon! Thanks again for the bike.

Love,
Kate

6. Birthday letter

To,
Mimi Rogers,
Sky Rise Apartments,
23 Grant Road,
Leeds, United Kingdom
May 14, 2008

Dear Daughter,

I would like to wish you a very Happy Birthday and many happy returns of the day. You have been the best daughter a father could have asked for.

I still remember the day you were born when I first held you in my arms at the hospital. You were this little adorable angel. That was the happiest day of my life. I have been a proud father since then. I still remember your first birthday celebrations when I had held your hands and helped you to cut the birthday cake. Twenty-five years have passed since then, but we still share the same bonding.

As a father I wish for your long life and a great future ahead. You may achieve success in whatever field you pursue. May all the happiness in the world be yours.

Your loving father,
Jimmy Rogers

7. Friendship letter

Dear friend,

Hello! How are you? I only hope that you are perfectly fine. I know that we now seldomly see each other but I assure you that I never forget you. It's been a while that we talked about our friendship so I wrote you this letter.

It's been a busy day with me here. My study is just fine. Everything is perfect and the only thing that do not have is you. But I know that our separation is just temporary. I have new classmates and they are cool just like you. If there is a chance I'll let them meet you so we could hang out and have a chat. My teachers are very good and we always discuss wonderful subjects.

My friend, I really miss you a lot and I also miss our good times together. Remember the last time we saw each other? Gosh, it is stuck in my memory. That was great!

I hope to hear from you soon. Take care and God Bless! I love you my friend!

Love,

Joan

8. Farewell letter

23rd May, 2009

Dear Anne,

How are you? I am writing to inform you that I will be soon moving out of the neighborhood. It was really good having you as a neighbor. I can't thank you enough for all the help and support you offered me during my tough times.

I will be shifting to Princeton area as it would be convenient for me in more ways than one. The house I will be moving into has an extra bedroom and it would always be a pleasure to have you with me, when you come over this side.

My E-mail and phone numbers remain the same, and I look forward to keeping in touch with you. I will keep you updated about my postal address soon.

Thank you for everything once again,

With Best Wishes,

Jane Harriet

Step 2

Work in groups of 3 to 4 and discuss the following questions.

1. What kind of relation do you find between the writer and the recipient in each letter?

2. What common features do you find in the language used in these letters?

3. What differences do you find in the language in letters 1, 2, 4, 5 and in letters 3, 6, 7, 8? Why?

4. What differences do you find in the organization of letters 1, 2, 4, 5 and in letters 3, 6, 7, 8?

   Letters 1, 2, 4, 5: _____

   Letters 3, 6, 7, 8: _____

5. How many parts can the body sections of letters 3, 6, 7, 8 be divided into? What role does each part play in the writing of the letter and in attaining the purpose of the letter? What kind of information is given in each part? Complete the table below.

Part	Role of the part	Content or information
1	Beginning part: Introduction	Introducing the background and the purpose of writing the letter
2		
3		

Step 3

Underline useful expressions in these letters and keep them in your notebook and mind.

Useful expression for different types of friendly/personal letters:

1. **Apology letters**
   - I am writing this letter to apologize for ...
   - I'm sorry about ... / it was all my fault. / I have no excuse for my behavior and ...
   - I wish you are able to forgive me for what I did so that I get a chance to show you that I am sorry for everything and we can move on.
   - I'd just like to apologize again for ...

2. **Congratulation letters**
   - How wonderful it is to know/hear that ... / congratulations!
   - Please accept my heartiest congratulations on your ...
   - I'm really proud of you.
   - Once again, my sincere congratulations on your ...

3. **Invitation letters**
   - I would like to take this opportunity to invite you to ...
   - ... , we have organized a party and you are one of the invited.
   - I hope you can find time to attend the ... celebration.
   - We are happily expecting the warmth of your presence.
   - Please RSVP by ... to ensure attendance.
   - Thank you and expect to see you soon.

4. **Letters of refusing an invitation**
   - Thank you for your invitation to ...
   - Unfortunately, I have already made other arrangements then and ...
   - Hope you have fun.

5. **Birthday letters**
   - I would like to wish you a very Happy Birthday and many happy returns of the day.
   - I wish for your long life and a great future ahead.
   - I pray for your good health on this special day. I also wish ...

---

6. **Thank-you letters**
   - I would like to thank you for the warm birthday wishes as well as ...
   - Thanks for ... ; it's just what I wanted.
   - Thank you once again for ...

7. **Farewell letters**
   - I am writing this letter to bid you farewell as I leave ... for ...
   - As you all know, very soon, I will be leaving ... to ...
   - It is sad that we will be farther from you.
   - Very soon I shall forward my contact details.
   - I look forward to keeping in touch with you.

8. **Friendship letters**
   - Hello! How are you? I only hope that you are perfectly fine.
   - My friend, I really miss you a lot and I also miss our good times together.
   - I hope to hear from you soon. Take care and God Bless!
   - Keep in touch dear friend!
   - See you soon!

TASK TWO
Writing Friendly/Personal Letters Properly

Step 1

Work in pairs. Choose two topics from the situations given below and practice writing two types of friendly/personal letters.

1. You invite one of your classmates to your birthday party.
2. You express your gratitude to your friend who helped you when you were ill.
3. You write to your best friend who studies in another city.
4. You write to your mother/father/any other family members to say happy birthday to him/her.
5. You write to your former teacher or classmate to say goodbye to him/her.

6. You congratulate your friend on his/her receiving an offer from Stanford University.

Follow the steps listed below in your writing.

Steps of writing a friendly/personal letter：

1. Include the recipient's address and the date (directly below the address) on the top left or right side of the letter, with a blank line beneath the date. (This part is optional.)

2. Write a friendly salutation, with the word "Dear" followed by the first name or title and the full name, depending on the relation between you and the recipient. Leave a blank line between the salutation and the main text of the letter.

3. Include introduction, body, and conclusion in the text of your letter, either in different paragraphs or directly in one short paragraph to make the letter brief and to the point.

4. Conclude with an appropriate closing, depending on your relation with the recipient, like *Sincerely*, *Yours*, *Love*, *Regards*, *Until next time*, *Talk to you soon*, etc.

5. Sign your name below the closing, with your first name or your full name.

ASSIGNMENTS

Choose two other topics from the situations given in TASK TWO, and write two other types of friendly/personal letters. Include different parts of the body section in different paragraphs and provide enough detailed information in your letters. Follow the steps listed in TASK TWO when writing your letters.

Module 14 Writing Different Types of Formal/Business Letters

When finishing the learning of this module,

Goal 1　I will know roles of different parts in the body section of a formal/business letter.

Goal 2　I will know some useful expressions in writing different formal/business letters.

Goal 3　I will know how to write different types of formal/business letters properly.

Section 2　Writing Letters for Practical Purposes · · · · · · · · · ·

TASK ONE

Understanding Roles of Different Parts in a Letter

Step 1

Read the following letters. Analyze the organization and language used in each letter.

1. University Application/Admission Letter

Clara

432 E, Drachmann

Tucson, AZ 85705

U. S. A

Marc Anthony

Department of Information Science

School of Science, Westwood University

462 B7, Down street

Phoenix, AZ 567898

U. S. A

Dear Mr. Anthony,

I am a graduate student in computers, from Wein and Leigh College. This letter is regarding the queries on admission process in your college; I have applied for the course of "Intelligent agents and systems" in your esteemed university.

I was the university topper and a gold medalist in neural networks in our college. I have also cleared GRE and TOEFL with an aggregate of 89% and a CGPA of about 8 on the scale of 10. I think I am eligible for the course because I have core knowledges in Artificial intelligence and Neural Networks. I am also proficient in Machine learning and expert systems. Kindly send me the further procedures in your college for admission after the group discussion round as I am shortlisted after the same. Do the needful and oblige.

Sincerely,

Clara
(Student)

2. Job Application/Cover Letter

527 West Ave.
Elmswood, CT 23865
October 28, 2004

Mr. Michael Black
Director of Human Resources
Global Answers
6542 Sioux Falls, NY

Dear Mr. Black:

It is with great interest that I am applying for the position of chief accountant. When I read the job description of your ad in the *New York Times* on August 12th, I felt that it was an ideal match with my career aspirations. I have always wanted to work for an outstanding company in the Fortune 500 such as Global Answers.

I believe that I am the ideal candidate for the position due to my extensive experience as an auditor for KPMG. At my current position at KPMG, I perform all of the same tasks that are described in your ad for the chief accountant position. In addition to that I have a reputation for being a hard worker who makes sure the job is done right the first time. My reports are always completed well ahead of the deadline.

Feel free to contact me and set up an interview at your earliest convenience. You can reach me by way of e-mail at KenJacobs@nadate.com or by way of phone at (555) 555-5555. I look forward to discussing with you my future with Global Answers.

Thanks for your time and consideration.

Sincerely,

(*Signature*)

Ken Jacobs

Enclosure: resume

3. Inquiry Letter

Mr. Steve Heyman
Adams Ave
Melbourne, FL 32935
March 14, 2010

Dr. Jennifer Davis
Florida Hospital
Titusville, FL 32780

Dear Dr. Davis,

I am a medicine student studying at California College. Next year, I need to take up internship at a hospital where I can gain practical experience and be exposed to actual medical cases. I have found your hospital to be one of the best where I can spend my internship and I would like to inquire whether you are accepting interns at the moment. I would also like to inquire about your requirements for application.

I am an exceptional student at my college and I hope that I would be accepted as one of your interns. I will be most willing to submit to your process for application. If you need to contact me, you can reach me at 321-259-5023.

Thank you. I hope for your swift action.

Respectfully,

Steve Heyman

4. Request Letter

Mycroft Westbury,
Arizona
29 April, 2000

Mr. John Stanhope,
Human Resource Manager,
CISCO Solutions,
Arizona, U. S. A

Dear Mr. Stanhope,

Allow me to introduce to you myself, Mycroft Westbury, the Senior Engineer in CISco Solutions. I have been in this position for more than five years now.

I have heard the news that the position of a Quality Analyst is vacant in the company from my peers. The purpose of my writing to you, sir, is to request you to transfer me to that position. I am well qualified for the post and also possess the relevant experience. Since I have been working with analysis and design, it will be well within my expertise arena. In this regard, I want to meet up with you personally to discuss the possibility, whenever it is convenient for you. I reckon that you would give my transfer a deserved thought.

Thanks and regards,

Mycroft Westbury

Senior Engineer

5. Apology Letter

September 9, 2010
Ms. Pamela Scott
Supervisor
Ink Magic, Inc.

Dear Ms. Scott:

I write this letter to express my apology for being tardy these past two days. My baby has been ill for one week now and I have had to give extra care for him until early morning before leaving for work. This morning, I had to bring him to the hospital due to a high fever and couldn't leave him with the caregiver right away.

I will make up for the lost time by staying for an extra two hours after my shift in the office to work for two days. If necessary, I will also accept additional workload. Although the cause of my tardiness was unexpected, I will not forget to immediately inform you about my situation should the same problem occur. I hope you accept my apologies.

Thank you. I am hoping for your kind consideration.

Warm regards,

Mary McGhee

Staff

6. Thank-you letter

March 18，2010
Mr. Jason Arnold
ABC Multinational Corp. Ltd.
12/3 Mayfair Lane，
Justatown，OH

Dear Jason，

I would take this opportunity to place on record my gratitude to endow me with the Business School Scholarship. I would like to thank you for providing me with this opportunity to pursue my higher studies at your institution.

My aim is to put in only my best efforts and add great value to your institution. I am determined to bring a difference in the world of business. I am sure about the capabilities of your Business School as it has churned out some of the brightest professionals in various aspects of business，be it entrepreneurs or executives. I am confident that with my abilities I will add more success to your record of laurels.

My gratitude once again for the scholarship provided.

Yours sincerely，

Roy Goldsmith

Student of Business Administration

Step 2

Work in groups of 3 to 4. Discuss the following questions and complete the table below with appropriate information from your discussion about the letters in Step 1.

1. What kind of relation do you find between the writer and the recipient in each letter? What differences do you find in the formats of formal/business letters in Step 1 and friendly/personal letters in Module 13?

2. What differences do you find in the salutations and the closings used in formal/ business letters in Step 1 and in friendly/personal letters in Module 13? Give

some examples.

3. What common features do you find in the language used in the letters in Step 1? What differences do you find in the language of these formal letters and the friendly letters in Module 13?

4. How many parts can the body sections of these formal letters be divided into? What role does each part play in the writing and in attaining the purpose of each letter?

5. What kind of information or details are provided in different parts of these formal letters, and for what purposes?

Part	Role	Content or information	Purpose
Beginning part		Letter 1: Self-introduction, purpose of writing Letter 2: Letter 3: Letter 4: Letter 5: Letter 6:	
Middle part		Letter 1: Letter 2: Letter 3: Letter 4: Letter 5: Letter 6:	
Ending part		Letter 1: Letter 2: Letter 3: Letter 4: Letter 5: Letter 6:	

Step 3

Underline useful expressions in these letters.

Useful expression for different types of formal/business letters:

1. **University application/admission letters**
   - I introduce myself as ... student from the ...
   - I am enclosing the filled-in application form to pursue my higher studies from ...
   - I think I am eligible for the course because ... ; I am also proficient in ...
   - I was a high level achiever at ... ; I was equally active in ... ; I have won awards in ...
   - I kindly hope that my application will be reviewed in favor by the board.

2. **Job application/cover letters**
   - I am ... and I am writing this letter to you as a cover to my application for the position...
   - It is with great interest that I am applying for the position of ...
   - I got to know about the vacancy of the post through a friend who ...
   - When I read the job description of your ad in ... , I felt that it was an ideal match with...
   - I believe that I am the ideal candidate for the position.
   - I will be looking forward to working for you and hearing from you.

3. **Inquiry letters**
   - I have found ... and I would like to inquire whether ...
   - I want to inquire the procedure I need to follow to be able to ...
   - I wish to inquire about your requirements and qualifications for application as well as the details of ...
   - It would be of great help to me if details are revealed to me for any possible future recruitment drive conducted in near future.
   - I hope for your prompt response on this matter.

4. **Request letters**
   - The purpose of my writing to you, sir is to request you to ...
   - In this regard I wish to meet you for an interview for...
   - I write to you to request you to consider my name for ...
   - I am looking forward to further correspondence from your side.
   - Thanks in advance for considering my request for ...

---

5. **Apology letters**
   - I write this letter to express my apology for ...
   - I would like to apologize for ...
   - I will make up for... ; I am willing to render ... as to make up for its effect on ...
   - Rest assured that you will be immediately notified if such circumstances happen again in the future.
   - I hope you accept my apologies.

6. **Thank-you letters**
   - I take this opportunity to thank you once again for ...
   - I would like to thank you for ...
   - I appreciate your support in ...
   - My gratitude once again for ...

TASK TWO
Writing Formal/Business Letters Properly

Step 1

Work in pairs. Choose two topics from the situations given below and practice writing formal/business letters.

1. You apply for an opportunity to study in a university through an exchange program.
2. You apply for a part-time job in a small company or as a tutor in summer vocation.
3. You inquire about a scholarship program of a university which has given you an offer.
4. You write to the Department of International Cooperation and Exchanges of XJTU and request an opportunity to study abroad as an international exchange student.
5. You write to your teacher to apologize for submitting your paper late.
6. You express gratitude to the company that conducted your interview for a vacancy.

Follow the steps listed below in your writing.

Steps of writing a formal/business letter:

1. Write your name and address at the top of your letter, left-aligned and single spaced.

2. Put the date directly below your address, left-aligned, with a blank line below the date.

3. Write the recipient's address, left-aligned, with the entire address followed by a blank line.

4. Begin the body of your letter with a polite salutation, left-aligned, and leave a blank line after it.

5. Write the main text, left-aligned, with a self-introduction and explanation of the purpose of your letter.

6. Follow the introduction with a longer body portion, which provides more information or specific details. Leave a blank line between every two paragraphs.

7. Include a conclusion part which sums things up at the end of the body section, with a blank line left after the final paragraph.

8. End your letter with a polite closing, left-aligned.

9. Type your name, left-aligned, three blank lines beneath the closing.

10. Write your job title or position, left-aligned, below your name when necessary.

11. Indicate any enclosure at the very end of your letter, left-aligned, by typing "Enclosure(s)" one line below your typed name and title. Indicate the number or details of the enclosures.

12. Sign your name after printing your letter, in between the closing and your typed name.

ASSIGNMENTS

Choose two other topics from the situations given in TASK TWO, work individually and write two other types of formal/business letters. Include different parts of the body section in different paragraphs and provide enough detailed information in your letters. Follow the steps listed above when writing your letters.

Module 15 Writing Different Types of E-mails

When finishing the learning of this module,

Goal 1   I will know the formats of formal/business and friendly/personal E-mails.

Goal 2   I will know the language and organization features of different types of E-mails.

Goal 3   I will know the steps of writing E-mails and things to notice when writing E-mails.

Section 2   Writing Letters for Practical Purposes · · · · · · · · · ·

TASK ONE

Understanding Formats of Different Types of E-mails

Step 1

Work in pairs. Read the following E-mails and answer the questions below.

1. When and to whom do people write E-mails, and for what purposes?

2. What different types of E-mails can you find in these examples?

3. What basic elements and formats do you find in these E-mails?

4. What language and organization features do you find in each type of E-mails?

E-mail 1

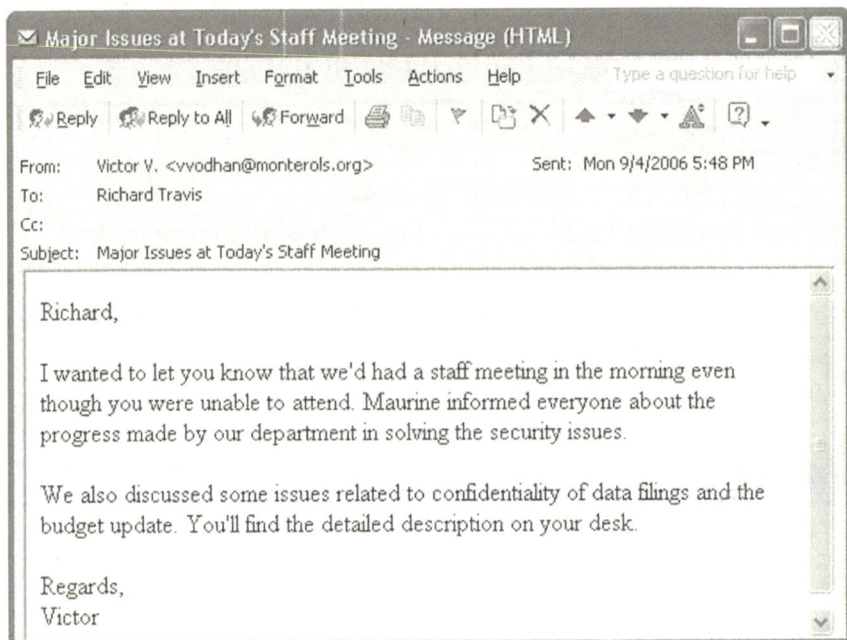

E-mail 2

Subject：materials for Wed. staff meeting

Hi，everyone—

For tomorrow's 3 p.m. staff meeting in the conference room，please bring 15 copies of the following materials：

- Your project calendar
- A one-page report describing your progress so far
- A list of goals for the next month
- Copies of any progress report messages you have sent to clients this past month

See you tomorrow.

Jane

E-mail 3

To: jjones@jonesofficesolutions.com

From: tmcaden@jonesofficesolutions.com

Subject: Meeting About New Internet Service Provider 1/8/2013

Mr. Jones,

I have been researching our choices for internet providers over the past week, and I wanted to update you on my progress. We have two options: H. C. Cable and Toll South. Both offer business plans, and I will go over the pricing of each plan at the meeting on Tuesday. Both of the options I listed have comparable speed and data usage offerings as well. I called your personal provider, GoGo Satellite, but they did not have any business offerings. They primarily do residential internet service.

I will talk with Joe and Susan in IT about these options and get their suggestions. I will also send out meeting requests to everyone, including Mr. Morris in operations. If you have any questions prior to the meeting, please let me know.

Respectfully,

Tina McAden

Administrative Assistant

Jones Office Solutions

http://www.jonesofficesolutions.com

(555) 124-5678

E-mail 4

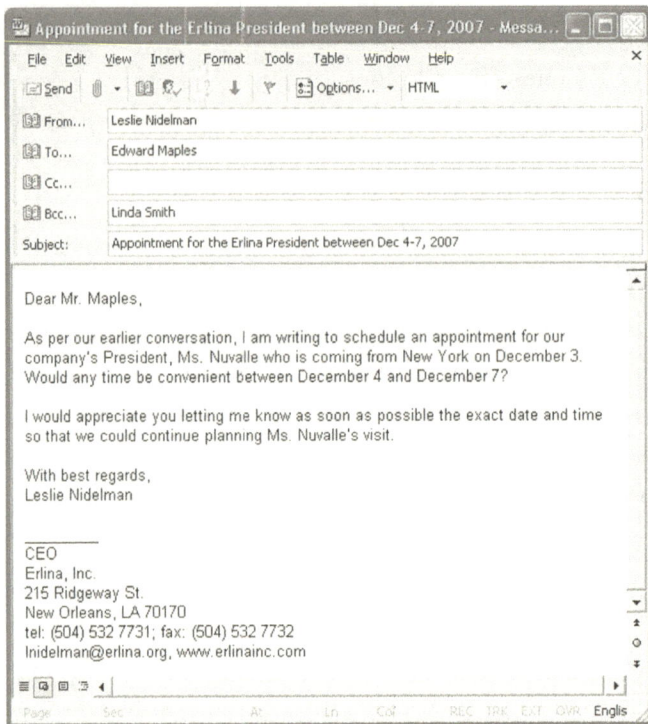

```
Appointment for the Erlina President between Dec 4-7, 2007 - Messa...

File   Edit   View   Insert   Format   Tools   Table   Window   Help          ×

Send  ▯  ▾  🖳 🖳  ?  ↓  ✧  🖳 Options...  ▾  HTML            ▾

From...   Leslie Nidelman

To...     Edward Maples

Cc...

Bcc...    Linda Smith

Subject:  Appointment for the Erlina President between Dec 4-7, 2007


Dear Mr. Maples,

As per our earlier conversation, I am writing to schedule an appointment for our
company's President, Ms. Nuvalle who is coming from New York on December 3.
Would any time be convenient between December 4 and December 7?

I would appreciate you letting me know as soon as possible the exact date and time
so that we could continue planning Ms. Nuvalle's visit.

With best regards,
Leslie Nidelman

_____
CEO
Erlina, Inc.
215 Ridgeway St.
New Orleans, LA 70170
tel: (504) 532 7731; fax: (504) 532 7732
lnidelman@erlina.org, www.erlinainc.com
```

Step 2

Work in groups of 3 to 4. Discuss the basic elements of E-mails, tick proper elements in the two different types of E-mails and fill in blanks with proper formats of different types of E-mails in the graph below. Some elements and blanks have been done for you as examples.

Elements	Format of formal/business E-mails	Format of informal/friendly E-mails
Sender's address Format	√ Yes ☐ No From:...	√ Yes ☐ No From:...
Recipient's address Format	☐ Yes ☐ No	√ Yes ☐ No To:...
Date Format	☐ Yes ☐ No	☐ Yes ☐ No

Elements	Format of formal/business E-mails		Format of informal/ friendly E-mails	
Subject line	☐ Yes	☐ No	☐ Yes	☐ No
Format				
Salutation	☐ Yes	☐ No	√ Yes	☐ No
Format			Left-aligned, first name followed by a comma	
Body	☐ Yes	☐ No	☐ Yes	☐ No
Format				
Closing	√ Yes	☐ No	☐ Yes	☐ No
Format	Formal, left aligned, followed by a comma			
Name and/or title	☐ Yes	☐ No	√ Yes	☐ No
Format			First name	
Contact information	☐ Yes	☐ No	☐ Yes	☐ No
Format				
Alignment	√ Yes	☐ No	☐ Yes	☐ No
Format	All elements left-aligned			
Indentation	☐ Yes	☐ No	☐ Yes	☐ No
Format				
Blank lines	√ Yes	☐ No	☐ Yes	☐ No
Format	Salutation/body, between two paragraphs, last paragraph/closing, closing/name/title/ address...			
Contractions	☐ Yes	☐ No	☐ Yes	☐ No
Format				
Abbreviations	☐ Yes	☐ No	☐ Yes	☐ No
Format				

Step 3

Go over the following examples. Discuss in pairs about the headers of the E-mails.

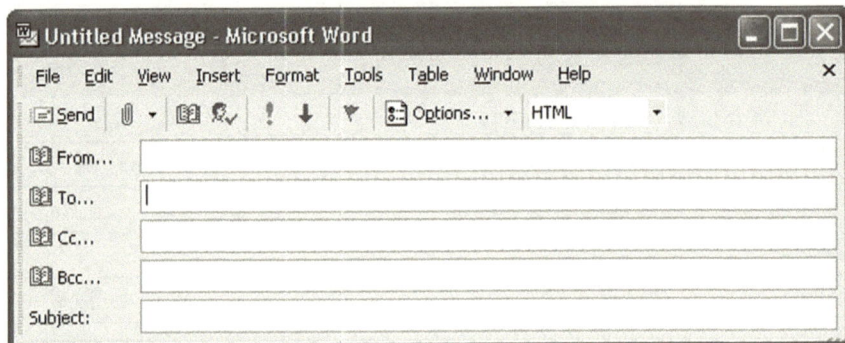

✉ Major Issues at Today's Staff Meeting - Message (HTML)

File	Edit	View	Insert	Format	Tools	Actions	Help	Type a question for help

Reply | Reply to All | Forward

From:　Victor Vodhan <vvodhan@monterols.org>　　　　Sent: Mon 9/4/2006 5:48 PM
To:　Richard Travis
Cc:
Subject:　Major Issues at Today's Staff Meeting

Untitled Message - Microsoft Word

File	Edit	View	Insert	Format	Tools	Table	Window	Help

Send | Options... ▾ HTML

From...
To...
Cc...
Bcc...
Subject:

Questions for discussion:

1. What basic elements are included in the header of an E-mail?

2. How should you make your E-mail address professional?

3. How should you use the **Cc:** or **Bcc:** fields properly when sending a message to more than one address?

4. How should you write a formal subject line?

TASK TWO
Language and Organization Features of E-mails

Step 1

Work in pairs. Summarize language and organization features in the two types of E-mails and tick proper items in the following graph. Add detailed information in the brackets when necessary.

Features	Formal/business E-mails	Informal/friendly E-mails
Language	☐ Formal ( ) ☐ Semi-formal ( ) ☐ Informal/casual ( )	☐ Formal ( ) ☐ Semi-formal ( ) ☐ Informal/casual ( )
Organization	☐ Introduction ( ) ☐ Body ( ) ☐ Conclusion ( )	☐ Introduction ( ) ☐ Body ( ) ☐ Conclusion ( )

Step 2

Work in pairs. Match the phrases 1 – 16 with the purposes in A – P.

1. That reminds me, ...	A. to finish the E-mail
2. Why don't we ...	B. to apologize
3. I'd better get going ...	C. to indicate the source of information
4. Thanks for your letter ...	D. to thank the person for writing
5. Please let me know ...	E. to begin the E-mail
6. I'm really sorry ...	F. to change the subject
7. Love,	G. to mention the attachment
8. Could you do something for me?	H. before signing the E-mail
9. My name is ... , the chairman of ...	I. to indicate the purpose of writing
10. Write soon ...	J. to ask a favor
11. Did you know that ...	K. to suggest or invite
12. I'm happy to hear that ...	L. to greet the recipient in general
13. I'm contacting you to ...	M. to ask for a reply
14. To whom it may concern ...	N. to introduce oneself
15. I obtained your website from ...	O. to share some information
16. I am attaching a copy of ...	P. to ask for a response

TASK THREE
Writing Different Types of E-mails Properly

Step 1

Choose one of the three topics and write an informal E-mail to a friend or family member. Follow the tips listed below in your writing.

1. Write to a friend you haven't seen for a long time. Tell him/her about what you have been doing and ask how he/she is and what he/she has been up to recently.

2. Write to a friend who you know has been having some problems. Ask him/her how he/she is doing and if you can help.

3. Write to your cousin and invite him/her to visit you on your campus. Briefly tell him/her about your university, as well as some details about your arrangement.

Tips in writing informal/friendly E-mails:

1. Begin with a brief yet accurate description of the subject of your E-mail in the subject field.

2. Start with a polite greeting or salutation in the actual text of the E-mail.

3. Include a blank line between the greeting and the body of your E-mail.

4. Type out the body of your E-mail, including the introduction, body, and conclusion. However, in writing an E-mail to a close friend, this kind of formatting may not be necessary.

5. Finish your E-mail with a closing salutation, or with words signaling the ending of the E-mail, or simply with your name if writing to a very close friend.

Step 2

Work in pairs. Review each other's E-mail, answer the following questions and give suggestions for him/her to improve his/her E-mail writing.

1. Does the E-mail have a proper header (sender's address, recipient's address and subject line)?
2. Is the subject line brief and clear? Why or why not?
3. How does the writer greet the recipient? Is the salutation used properly?
4. Is the content of the body section brief, concise and clear? Why or why not?
5. Does the writer begin, continue and end the body section properly? Why?
6. How does the writer close at the end? Does the writer sign off properly?
7. Are blank lines, commas and alignment used properly in his/her E-mail?
8. Are there spelling, capitalization, punctuation or grammar mistakes?

Step 3

Work in groups of 3 to 4. Discuss questions below about writing formal E-mails.

1. How should you use a proper salutation (title and name) in writing a formal E-mail?

_____

2. What should you write in different parts of the body section of a formal E mail?

_____

3. What language should you use in writing a formal E-mail? Give some examples.

_____

4. What fonts and sizes should you choose when writing a formal E-mail?

_____

5. How should you sign off properly at the end of a formal E-mail?

_____

6. What can also be included under your name in a formal E-mail, and in what format?

_____

7. What should you pay attention to when attaching files in your E-mail?

_____

8. What kind of information should not be included in an E-mail?

_____

9. What should you check before you finally send your E-mail?

_____

ASSIGNMENTS

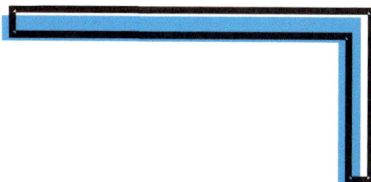

Choose one of the following topics and write a formal E-mail. Follow the steps and the format introduced in TASK THREE and also notice the E-mail etiquettes listed on the next page.

- You ask your teacher to write a recommendation letter to help you apply for a university.
- You write to the president of Xi'an Jiaotong University (XJTU) to give suggestions about certain problems shown in the teaching of students in the Honored Youth Program (少年班项目).
- You express your gratitude to someone who helped you a lot in doing something in the past.
- You apologize to someone for doing something wrong and causing problems.
- You write to your teacher to ask for a chance of having a make-up test due to your illness.

E-mail etiquettes: Show RESPECT to the person you are communicating with.

1. Address your E-mail to the specific person your E-mail is intended for instead of using "reply to all" or "forward to all" by mistake.

2. Use the Bcc (blind carbon copy) function of E-mails to hide recipients' E-mail addresses if you don't intend to have people's E-mail addresses known by others.

3. Avoid leaving the subject field empty or simply putting "Re:" as the subject line. Write an honest and specific subject heading that reflects your E-mail message.

4. Include the message you reply to in your sent message to help people know what you are talking about.

5. Keep your E-mail brief and concise, with all the necessary information provided upfront.

6. To avoid formatting issues, provide a website link if you want to copy an entire web page.

7. Avoid using abbreviations in formal E-mails or unknown abbreviations in friendly E-mails.

8. Avoid spelling mistakes, and avoid typing all words in capitals or lower cases.

9. Consider the size and format of your attachment if you have to send one in your E-mail.

10. Avoid requesting delivery and read receipts which could be unreliable and annoying, and avoid sending angry E-mails which may probably cause trouble.

11. Reread, check and edit before you finally send your E-mail.

12. Send your E-mail at an appropriate time if it may affect the recipient's judgment on you.

List of Sources

　　本书在编写时，为了保证语言纯正地道，我们参考了部分来源于国内外网站的语句和文章段落，在此罗列清单，并对原作者表示感谢。

http://blog. sina. com. cn/s/blog_51d7e597010125xh. html

http://cn. bing. com/images/search? q = comparison + and + contrast + paragraph&qpvt = comparison+and+contrast+paragraph&FORM=IGRE

http://colelearning. net/rw_wb/module5/page10. html

http://eduventure. ca/CauseEffect. pptx

http://english120. pbworks. com/w/page/19006810/cause%20and%20effect%20paragraphs

http://english120. pbworks. com/w/page/19006816/classification%20paragraphsSmoking

http://english120. pbworks. com/w/page/19006833/contrast%20and%20comparison%20paragraph

http://english120. pbworks. com/w/page/19006835/contrast%20paragraph

http://english120. pbworks. com/w/page/19006850/definition%20paragraphs

http://english120. pbworks. com/w/page/19006987/narrative%20paragraphs

http://english120. pbworks. com/w/page/19007022/process%20paragraph

http://kedatgym204. wikispaces. com/file/view/exercises_on_paragraph_writing. pdf

http://patternbasedwriting. com/elementary_writing_success/paragraph-examples

http://www. beaconlearningcenter. com/documents/888_01. pdf

http://www. doc88. com/p-142571493561. html

http://www. docin. com/p-1054040078. html

http://www. preservearticles. com/201107149072/list-of-six-sample-paragraphs-for-middle-school-students.html

http://www. savvy-business-correspondence. com/EmailBasics. html

http://www. savvy-business-correspondence. com/EmailEtiquette. html

http://zxq0913. blog. 163. com/blog/static/164738100201082104936380/

https://eslflow. com/descriptive-paragraphs-worksheet. html

https://k12. thoughtfullearning. com/studentmodels/friendship

https://lanxicy. com/read/3c1c0ff9f3b9d5be08c62bdd. html

https://lanxicy. com/read/5757fb5824854eb1f01efca3. html

https://lanxicy. com/read/af5228267d6429654eb2ed17. html

https://max.book118.com/html/2016/1105/61382159.shtm

https://max.book118.com/html/2017/1102/138578725.shtm

https://medlineplus.gov/smoking.html

https://oup.useremarkable.com/production/images/uploads/3686/original/uk_sample_informal-letter.pdf

https://patternbasedwriting.com/elementary_writing_success/paragraph-examples/

http://english120.pbworks.com/w/page/19006987/narrative%20paragraphs

https://web2.uvcs.uvic.ca/elc/sample/intermediate/unit2/u2_e2e.htm

https://web2.uvcs.uvic.ca/elc/sample/intermediate/unit2/u2_ex1.htm

https://web2.uvcs.uvic.ca/elc/sample/intermediate/unit2/u2_ex2.htm

https://wenku.baidu.com/view/439d721fc5da50e2524d7fc9.html?sxts=1547782239471

https://wenku.baidu.com/view/491608c805087632311212a2.html?from=search

https://wenku.baidu.com/view/5293ba038e9951e79a892750.html

https://wenku.baidu.com/view/776ae0fd5fbfc77da269b1bb.html

https://wenku.baidu.com/view/8869239d3186bceb19e8bbfd.html?from=search

https://wenku.baidu.com/view/922bf3cade80d4d8d05a4f46.html

https://wenku.baidu.com/view/ad9d891b6bd97f192279e990.html

https://wenku.baidu.com/view/afc30cb519e8b8f67c1cb9a1.html

https://wenku.baidu.com/view/d996d0c58762caaedd33d467.html?rec_flag=default&sxts=1533807184810

https://wenku.baidu.com/view/f33d383c0b4c2e3f57276329.html?sxts=1532851614939

https://writingcenter.unc.edu/tips-and-tools/effective-e-mail-communication/

https://www.bridgeport.edu/life/campus-activities/

https://www.cdc.gov/flu/about/disease/spread.htm

https://www.csun.edu/sites/default/files/Auerbach-Handout-Paragraph-Writing-Examples.pdf

https://www.douban.com/note/499829477/

https://www.ereadingworksheets.com/text-structure-worksheets/identifying-text-structure-2-answers.html

https://www.lanxicy.com/read/aafb82a968bb0a70ff1dae59.html

https://www.letterwritingguide.com/sampleapologypersonal.htm

https://www.letterwritingguide.com/samplecoverletter.htm

https://www.letterwritingguide.com/sampleinvitationbusiness.htm

https://www.letterwritingguide.com/sampleinvitationpersonal.htm

https://www.letterwritingguide.com/thankyounotesample.htm

https://www.oupcanada.com/higher_education/companion/literature/9780195425154/eng_135/

quiz_transitions. html

https://www. sampleletters. org/apology-letter-for-tardiness. html

https://www. sampleletters. org/birthday-letter-to-a-daughter. html

https://www. sampleletters. org/internship-inquiry-letter. html

https://www. sampleletters. org/sample-farewell-letter. html

https://www. sampleletters. org/sample-friendship-letter. html

https://www. sampleletters. org/sample-thank-you-letter. html

https://www. sampleletters. org/transfer-request-letter. html

https://www. sampleletters. org/university-admission-letter. html

https://www. sdcity. edu/Portals/0/CMS_Editors/EnglishCenter/English%20Center%20documents/
   The%20Well-Developed%20Paragraph. pdf

https://www. thoughtco. com/model-descriptive-paragraphs-1690573

https://www. thoughtco. com/narrating-things-happening-over-time-1212346

https://www. thoughtco. com/writing-an-informal-letter-1212384

https://www. wikihow. com/Sample/Formal-Email-to-Boss

https://www. wikihow. com/Write-a-Descriptive-Paragraph

https://www. writing. com/main/view_item/item_id/927399-How-To-Write-A-Good-Paragraph